Including All Of Us

Including All Of Us

An Early Childhood Curriculum About Disability

By Merle Froschl
Linda Colón
Ellen Rubin
Barbara Sprung

Developed by Project Inclusive
Educational Equity Concepts, Inc.
New York, 1984

Women's Educational Equity Act Program
U.S. Department of Education
T.H. Bell, Secretary

Cover and book design by Jim Anderson.

Photographs by Neil M. Shively.

Photographs were taken at the White Plains (NY) Child Day Care Association, Inc. and the Spring Creek Early Childhood Center, Brooklyn, New York.

On the cover: Suzy, a "New Friend" doll, with children at the White Plains Child Day Care Association.

Typeset by Jiffy Jenie Printing Center, Inc., Centereach, N.Y.

Printed by Arcata Graphics/Fairfield, Fairfield, PA.

Second printing, July 1986.

While the anecdotes described throughout this guide are real, the names of the people used are fictional.

Copyright © 1984 by Educational Equity Concepts, Inc.
All rights reserved under International and Pan-American Copyright Conventions.
Published by Educational Equity Concepts, Inc.,
New York, New York.
Printed in the U.S.A.
Distributed by Gryphon House, Inc., 3706 Otis Street, P.O. Box 275, Mt. Rainier, MD 20712.

Library of Congress Cataloging in Publication Data
Main entry under title:

Including all of us.

"Developed by Project Inclusive, Educational Equity Concepts."
    Bibliography: p.
    1. Education, Preschool—New York (State)—White Plains—Curricula.   2. Prejudices in children—New York (State)—White Plains.   3. Attitude change in children—New York (State)—White Plains.
4. Text-book bias—New York (State)—White Plains.
5. Educational equalization—New York (State)—White Plains.   6. Handicapped in literature—Bibliography.   7. Handicapped—Juvenile literature—Bibliography.   I. Froschl, Merle.   II. Educational Equity Concepts (New York, N.Y.)
LB1140.245.W48I53   1985   372.19   84-26022
ISBN 0-931629-00-4 (pbk.)

Discrimination Prohibited: No person in the United States shall, on the grounds of race, color or national origin, be excluded from participation in, be denied the benefits of, or be subjected to discrimination under any program or activity receiving Federal financial assistance, or be so treated on the basis of sex under most education programs or activities receiving Federal assistance.

The activity which is the subject of this report was produced under a grant from the U.S. Department of Education, under the auspices of the Women's Educational Equity Act. Opinions expressed herein do not necessarily reflect the position or policy of the Department, and no official endorsement should be inferred.

Acknowledgments

Project Inclusive wishes to thank each and every person who helped to create this curriculum guide. The children who participated in the pilot testing of the curriculum receive our greatest appreciation. They truly made the ideas and materials come to life.

Special thanks are extended to the White Plains Child Day Care Association for their enthusiasm and cooperation during the pilot testing. Our appreciation to Lyn Yanuck, Director; Martha Brogan, Educational Director; Marie Baxter, Pat Cartwright-Foendoe, and Sharon Rogers, Teachers; Sara Bannister, Carmen Calderon, Pamela Henry, and Lillian Herrick, Assistant Teachers; and the entire staff for their willingness to be flexible and provide class coverage.

We also would like to acknowledge the role of the larger school community in the success of the pilot testing: The White Plains Bus Company and its drivers for demonstrating the accessibility of a school bus to the children, Brian Wallach for spending time in the classes and answering children's questions, Harold Ward for turning a wagon into a "wheelchair" that the children could use, and, of course, all the parents who shared their children's reactions with us and proved that an inclusive curriculum strengthens home and school communication.

Many thanks, too, to Pat Greenwald, Director, and the staff of the Spring Creek Early Childhood Center in Brooklyn, New York. They allowed us to photograph the children, and the success of their mainstreaming effort was an inspiration to all of us.

We would like to give special recognition to the role played by Patricia B. Campbell in the development of this guide. Dr. Campbell, a noted educator and researcher, was the evaluator for the project and was involved from its inception. In addition to assessing the effectiveness of the curricular activities, she helped to develop and pilot test the curriculum, and read and commented on the draft of the guide.

We also wish to thank Project Inclusive's senior consultants who, through their help in the development of this project, their valuable comments on the draft of the manuscript, and all their advocacy work for children and adults with disabilities, have provided more substantive ideas than can be adequately acknowledged here. They are: Carrie Cheek, Assistant Director, New York University Head Start Regional Resource Support Center, Early Childhood Specialist, New York, New York; Katherine J. Corbett, disability rights activist and former project coordinator, Disabled Women's Educational Equity Project, Disability Rights Education and Defense Fund, Inc. (DREDF), Berkeley, California; Susan Quinby, Associate Director, Office for

Disabled Students, Barnard College, New York, New York; Judith Rothschild-Stolberg, Department Head, Human Services and Education, School of Continuing Education, New York University, New York, New York; and Jan Calderón Yocum, Executive Director, El Centro Rosemount, Washington, D.C.

We wish to thank as well the educators who, in addition to the senior consultants, read and validated the draft of this guide. Their thoughtful and valuable suggestions, from diverse backgrounds and perspectives, have been incorporated into this final version wherever possible. They are: Beryle Banfield, President, Council on Interracial Books for Children and Project Director, New York University Metro Center; Marie Baxter, Teacher, White Plains Child Day Care Association; Martha Brogan, Educational Director, White Plains Child Day Care Association; Pat Cartwright-Foendoe, Teacher, White Plains Child Day Care Association; Jamila Colón, Teacher, P.S. 87; Pat Greenwald, Director, Spring Creek Early Childhood Center; Peggy Hlibok, Coordinator, Special School of the Future, Edward R. Murrow High School; Sharon Rogers, Teacher, White Plains Child Day Care Association; Emily Strauss-Watson, Speech Pathologist, Ramsey (New Jersey) Board of Education; and Lyn Yanuck, Director, White Plains Child Day Care Association.

The following people provided reader services: Theresa Furman, Maryann Mazzacaro, Elise Teichert, and Gail Berman Weingram. For help with translation, we would like to thank Francesca D'Andrea, Rami Gertler, Joy Tong, Wabwoba M. Walinywa, and Alexandra Weinbaum. Thanks to Mel Carter and Barbara Olmert of the National Association for the Deaf for their assistance in finding and granting permission to reproduce various words in American Sign Language. A special note of thanks to the people who provided us with canes, hearing aids, glasses, and glasses frames free of charge. These include many local merchants and community service providers, in particular, the Jewish Guild for the Blind and the Lexington School for the Deaf. We would like to give special recognition to the Chapel Hill Training Outreach Project, developers of the "New Friend" dolls that proved to be a pivotal part of this curriculum.

Special thanks go to Jim Anderson for graphic design of the book, to Mary Allison who copyedited the manuscript, to Joni Miller for typing the manuscript in its many evolutions, and to Neil Shively who took the photographs. They all worked intensively, skillfully, and under pressing deadlines.

Finally, we wish to acknowledge that Project Inclusive was made possible by a grant from the Women's Educational Equity Act Program, U.S. Department of Education. We thank the staff of the program for their work, we especially want to thank our program officer, John Fiegel, for his encouragement and support throughout.

Contents

Preface

Including All of Us is a guide for creating an early childhood curriculum that is "inclusive," one that is nonsexist, multicultural, and incorporates both images and actual role models of children and adults with disabilities. An "inclusive" curriculum provides opportunities for every child to develop her or his full potential unhampered by stereotyped expectations regarding sex, race, or disability.

Such an approach extends early childhood learning in significant ways. It fosters children's cognitive, social, and emotional growth by expanding their world view to include people with disabilities and by teaching appreciation of and respect for human differences. By making the topic of disability accessible to children, parents, and teachers, the guide increases parent/child and home/school communication.

Including All of Us celebrates individual differences and encourages the development of a positive self-image. By encompassing fundamental principles of child development and educational equity, this early childhood curriculum benefits all children.

History of Project Inclusive

In the Fall of 1983, Educational Equity Concepts, Inc. initiated Project Inclusive: An Equity Approach to Early Childhood Education, under a grant from the U.S. Department of Education, Women's Educational Equity Act Program. Educational Equity Concepts is a national, non-profit organization founded in 1982 to create for children and adults educational programs and materials that are free of sex, race/ethnic, and disability bias. Through this effort, the organization's goal is to eliminate stereotypes and maximize opportunities for all children.

Project Inclusive proposed to address a crucial area that largely has been overlooked in the effort to mainstream children with disabilities—the integration of actual role models as well as images of children and adults with disabilities into the classroom environment and curriculum.

The project goal was to produce an "inclusive" early childhood curriculum guide, pre-k through first grade. An "inclusive" curriculum is one that has been expanded to incorporate issues of sex, race, and disability into the early childhood classroom. To accomplish this goal, the work of the project was divided into three phases: planning and development, pilot testing, and production of the guide.

PLANNING AND DEVELOPMENT

The planning and development phase involved a materials search, selection of the pilot site, inservice training, and curriculum development.

Materials Search

During the first two months of the project, an intensive search for inclusive materials was conducted, and this continued throughout the project. Project staff searched for materials that were not sex or race stereotyped and that portrayed positive images of children and adults with disabilities. Such a search was needed because inclusive materials are not widely known, and many are not yet part of most early childhood programs. The result of the search was a collection of outstanding early childhood materials including classroom materials, children's books, and background readings for teachers and parents that became an integral part of the curriculum development for Project Inclusive. (For a complete listing of available materials, see Resources section of this guide.)

Pilot Site

The White Plains (New York) Child Day Care Association, Inc., agreed to serve as the pilot site for the development and testing of the inclusive curriculum. Serving 250 children in both Head Start and day care, the White Plains Child Day Care Association provided a diverse population of children, teachers, and parents in terms of race/ethnicity, socioeconomic status, and disability. It also had a staff committed to quality education for all children and to the goals of Project Inclusive. The staff's cooperation and hard work were a major contribution to the success of the project. Three classes—three-year-olds, four-year-olds, and five-year-olds—pilot tested the curricular activities.

Inservice Training

An important component of the planning and development phase was inservice training for teachers and assistants. The purpose of these sessions was two-fold: first, to raise awareness of the issues of sex, race, and disability bias, and second, to establish what kinds of resources teachers and assistants would need to implement the curriculum. The training sessions focused on how attitudes are reflected in one's interactions with children, in one's use or choice of language, and in the selection of early childhood classroom materials. Teachers role played classroom situations, discussed actual incidences of discrimination, and reviewed and compared classroom materials. Training took place over the course of three weeks, during which time teachers and project staff exchanged information and ideas and discussed the background readings provided for teachers.

Curriculum Development
Because the goal of Project Inclusive was to develop curriculum that would extend from the existing curriculum, it was important to gather information on each class such as: routine activities, mandatory and voluntary activities, classroom set-up, curriculum covered, curriculum planned, expected trips, and so forth. From the information gathered, three curriculum areas were chosen for development: Same/Different, Body Parts, and Transportation. A meeting with teachers, assistants, and project staff generated ideas for expanding these three curriculum areas and, using the resources gathered during the materials search, the activities were developed. Same/Different was expanded to include hearing impairment, Body Parts to include visual impairment, and Transportation to include mobility impairment. Six activities were developed for each curriculum area. In addition, teachers and assistants were asked to expand on their own ideas as they pilot tested the activities as well as encouraged to utilize community resources, e.g., inviting a person with a disability to visit the class.

PILOT TESTING

The pilot testing of the curriculum took place over a two-month period, April-May 1984. Generally, teachers introduced two activities in each classroom per week. Evaluation was an integral and ongoing part of every phase of the pilot testing. The evaluation design included the development of observation forms and questionnaires to assess the effectiveness of the curriculum as well as its interest, usability, completeness, and accuracy.

Interviews were conducted with participating teachers and children by the project evaluator both at the beginning and end of the pilot testing, and ongoing records were kept throughout the pilot testing. To facilitate the gathering of data for evaluation and to collect first-hand anecdotes, several steps were taken: 1) all activities were tape-recorded, 2) teachers used observation forms to record their observations of children using the resource materials, and 3) a project staff member observed each of the classrooms on a weekly basis. Also, project staff members met weekly with teachers and assistants. At these weekly meetings, teachers and assistants described what happened when they introduced the activities in each of their classes, and discussions focused on enhancing the activities and developing new ideas.

Project Inclusive agreed with the Head Start philosophy that parents be kept informed of and be encouraged to participate in their children's educational experiences. To reach parents, most of whom worked outside the home during the day, a letter was sent home near the beginning of the project with a description of some of the activities that were being introduced in the children's classes. Parents were encouraged to call or drop in to talk to teachers and project staff.

A parents' meeting was held during which the children's work and the resource materials were displayed. The staff commented that the parent turnout was extraordinary—well above the usual parent participation. Of the 50 families whose children participated in the pilot testing, 30 were represented at the meeting. Many children were represented by grandmothers, mothers, foster mothers, and fathers. Teachers and assistants from each classroom highlighted some of the children's and their own experiences. Parents, in turn, shared some of the interactions they had with their children, which were directly related to the project.

One father mentioned that "my son has been coming home different nights mentioning things, but until I heard everything tonight, I hadn't put it all together. He told me about the wheelchair and about the guide dog." Another parent added, "Sheryl came home and taught me the sign for growing, and we say goodnight in sign language." Parents' and teachers' enthusiasm and comments reinforced the project's belief in the positive influence an inclusive environment can have on all children and adults.

PRODUCTION OF THE GUIDE

Including All of Us: An Early Childhood Curriculum About Disability incorporates the activities developed and information gathered during months of planning, development, and pilot testing. It contains activities, approaches, and resources to assist teachers and parents as they begin to create an inclusive environment for children ages three to five. It is the intention of Project Inclusive that this guide expand children's experiences to include nonstereotyped images and role models of people of color and people with disabilities. It is hoped that educators will take this effort a step further and extend it to all curriculum areas in early childhood programs. Through this effort, an inclusive environment will become a part of all children's educational experiences so they will not be limited in terms of sex, race/ethnic background, or disability.

Introduction

At a parent meeting a father of a four-year-old recounted:

> I was surprised at how readily Jessie comprehended the concept of sign language. One evening my wife was putting Jessie to bed. As my wife kissed her good-night, Jessie kept moving her hands and saying, "I'm trying to tell you something." My wife thought Jessie was going through her usual bedtime stalling tactics. In fact, she was signing "I love you" to her mommy.

This parent was sharing an anecdote about his child's reaction to Project Inclusive.

It points out why it is important to introduce the concept of disability at the beginning of a child's education. Think back to when you were a child. If you were not disabled yourself, did you know anyone who was? How were you taught to react to that person? Were you taught never to stare? Were you told to be extraordinarily kind? Were you afraid of people who were deaf or blind or who used wheelchairs or crutches? Did you shun or mock children and adults who were mentally retarded or emotionally disturbed?

For many people when they were children, opportunities to know people with disabilities were extremely limited. Only if a family member was disabled was there person-to-person interaction on an everyday basis. Society taught that people with disabilities were "special," and parents and others gave societal clues about how "they" should be treated. For many people, a person's disability took precedence; and that one difference became more important than all the similarities. Typically, people were divided into "them" and "us," and instead of forming friendships, barriers were created.

Adults who were disabled as children can appreciate the importance of incorporating disability into the early childhood environment. Children with disabilities often were deprived of positive adult role models, which had a serious effect on their own self-image. Children with disabilities bore the brunt of nondisabled people's attitudes and behaviors, and as a result, many experienced isolated and lonely childhoods. The barriers set up by the nondisabled society denied social interaction, educational opportunities, independence, and the chance to develop one's full potential. This waste of human ability is an immeasurable loss for everyone.

DISABILITY RIGHTS LEGISLATION

In the last decade, thanks to the tireless work of disability rights advocates, some important legislation has been passed. In 1973 a major piece of legislation for people with disabilities—Section 504 of the Vocational Rehabilitation Act—was passed; it prohibits discrimination on the basis of disability in all federally financed and assisted programs. Even earlier, in 1972, in amendments to the Economic Opportunities Act, Congress mandated that at least ten percent of the children enrolled in Head Start programs have disabilities encompassing orthopedic, speech, hearing, visual, intellectual, or emotional impairments ranging from mild to severe. And in 1975, Public Law 94-142—The Education of All Handicapped Children Act—was enacted; it declares that all children with disabilities are entitled to a free, appropriate education in the "least restrictive" environment.

As a result, adults and children with disabilities are entering the mainstream of society in unprecedented numbers. Increases in accessible transportation, public places, and worksites have meant that many adults who are disabled can actively participate in the social, political, and economic life of the society. Public Law 94-142 has meant that children with disabilities can expect the same educational opportunities as their nondisabled peers. The Head Start mandate has brought children with disabilities into mainstreamed classrooms at a very early age, and a network of Resource Access Projects (RAPS) provides training and technical assistance to facilitate the effort.

PROVIDING ROLE MODELS

Civil rights legislation, Head Start, the Resource Access Projects, and the training and curricular materials they have produced (see Resources section) have made a difference. Undeniably, there have been positive gains in the past decade, but much more needs to be done. As children with disabilities move into the educational mainstream, some changes need to take place. As with all children, children with disabilities need to see themselves reflected in the world around them, in pictures, in toys, in classroom materials, and in books. Interaction with positive role models should be a part of every child's education. For children with disabilities, this has been a serious omission. Without such role models, adults with disabilities report that as children they believed that 1) they would outgrow their disability, or 2) they would die and not grow up. While these attitudes may seem far-fetched, one only has to remember the limited frames of reference and the very literal learning styles of young children to understand how such conclusions could be reached.

Through positive role-model experiences and through disability-related curricular activities and materials, children (disabled and nondisabled) are able to express their feelings about disability, gain new information, and expand their world view. Through familiarity and knowledge comes acceptance of, respect for, and comfort with human differences.

It may seem like a simple task to change the early childhood classroom environment to provide these essential role-model experiences for children. But, even in the 1980s, after nearly a decade of mainstreaming efforts on the part of educators and disability rights advocates, it is still the "norm" to walk into mainstreamed, nonmainstreamed, and special education classrooms at every level of education and see virtually no representation of children or adults with disabilities. In one survey conducted in 1980 by Project R.E.E.D. (Resources on Educational Equity for the Disabled), a program funded by the Women's Educational Equity Act, all types of programs were visited to look for books, hands-on materials, posters, photographs, and actual role models of children and adults with disabilities. Except for an occasional book about a disabled child (not necessarily one with a positive image), the observers found nothing—not one poster, puppet, puzzle, or any other material that helped children, both disabled and nondisabled, understand disability as part of life.

BECOMING AWARE OF STEREOTYPES BASED ON DISABILITY

The problem is not necessarily a lack of resources, rather it is something even more fundamental—a lack of awareness. In the recent past, many educators have taken steps to eliminate racial and ethnic stereotypes from programs and materials. Others have focused on removing the limiting effects of sex-role stereotyping from the early childhood environment. A few educators have tried to eliminate negative images regarding age and class as well as sex, race, and ethnicity stereotypes. They have made serious attempts to create non-stereotyped learning environments, realizing that *any* kind of bias limits the growth and development of children. What for the most part has gone unrecognized, however, is that stereotyping on the basis of disability, too, limits children's potential and needs to be addressed from the beginning of the educational process. Only through such a comprehensive approach can educational equity for all children become a reality.

Most nondisabled people have been socialized not to think about disability unless it directly affects them or a close family member. When asked to examine their own attitudes about disability, nondisabled people's first reactions are to appear comfortable and enlightened and to keep their fears and discomforts well hidden from view. But most people who are not disabled have to some degree internalized society's myths and stereotyped attitudes toward people with disabilities. If young children are to be helped to understand and accept disability as one of many human differences, those of us who interact with children as teachers, aides, administrators, volunteers, or as parents need to examine our own attitudes and understand how they were formed.

All people, disabled or nondisabled, need to go through a similar process of exploration. The experiences and attitudes brought to the issue of disability will, of course, be different depending on personal experiences, but the opportunity to discuss feelings and to think about one's own attitudes is an essential first step. Too often, educators who are disabled have felt the need to hide their disability because of the stigma society has placed on it. One such case was a day-care director who for years hid her dual hearing aids behind large earrings and an elaborate hairdo. When she finally did reveal them to the children in her center, she freed the children to talk about family members who also were hearing impaired.

One way to examine one's own attitudes is to discuss stereotyping as experienced by others. For example, during the pilot testing, participating teachers, assistant teachers, and classroom aides were asked to react to vignettes based on actual incidents of disability bias. One vignette described a class trip taken by a group of preschoolers who were blind to a department store to visit Santa Claus. While waiting on line, teachers and children overhead an adult say, "They shouldn't bring those children in here. They spoil Christmas for everyone." As one might expect, the teachers participating in the training reacted with indignation and said they certainly would have confronted such an insensitive person.

After discussing other vignettes, teachers were asked to role play a situation in which they confronted a colleague who has derogatorily referred to a child as a "cripple." While it had been fairly easy and very satisfying during earlier discussions to talk about being straightforward in addressing disability bias, when it came to actually doing so during the role play, participants became uncomfortable and were unable to be as direct and honest as they had expected.

Awareness experiences such as these help one gain insights into the complexities of addressing stereotyped attitudes in oneself as well as in others. Without such opportunities, it is hard to know how one will react in actual situations. Through discussions with peers, however, when able to ask questions and voice concerns, one can become more comfortable with the issues and more honest in confronting one's own attitudes. Children, too, both disabled and nondisabled, when learning about disability, need to feel comfortable enough to ask questions and openly voice their concerns. In short, if an inclusive environment is the goal of an early childhood center, the topic of disability must be made accessible to staff, to children, and to parents.

LANGUAGE BIAS

Sex, race, and disability stereotyping in language is very pervasive and can have a negative effect on a person's self-image. Words and expressions of speech instantly convey individual and/or societal prejudices toward specific groups. For example, sexist language, such as calling a woman of any age "girl" and using "he" as a generic pronoun, thereby denying the existence of over one-half of the human race, serves to make girls and women into second class citizens who never quite grow up. Racist stereotypes such as referring to a Black man of any age as "boy" or to a Black woman as "the girl" serve to derogate and deny full personhood.

Disability stereotyping is reflected in such words as "cripple," which is derived from "creep," and "handicapped," which is a begging term meaning "cap-in-hand." Such words convey helplessness and dependency. They conjure up feelings of pity rather than respect. Many idioms and expressions of speech still widely in use also reflect lack of sensitivity and negative attitudes toward people with disabilities. For example, "the blind leading the blind" is used to describe people who don't seem to know what they are doing, and "limping along" is a common way to describe someone who is in an uncertain financial situation.

For the most part, teachers everywhere have become quite sensitive to racial and ethnic slurs and do not allow children to use them as epithets in the classroom. Many have reported, however, that except for the most blatant sexist and disability-related slurs—taunting boys by calling them "girls" or children calling each other "retards" as an insult—they are much less aware of sex and disability bias in language. For example, during the pilot testing, teachers remarked that they usually referred to pet animals and animal storybook characters as "he," and frequently used terms like firemen, policemen, and mailmen, thereby perpetuating the notion that all these jobs are held only by men. Teachers also acknowledged that they needed to become more aware of the expressions they used that might convey disability bias, e.g., saying someone is "confined" to a wheelchair, not realizing that for persons who have a mobility impairment, a wheelchair is a liberating vehicle that allows them to move around, or referring to someone as a "victim of" or "suffering from" cerebral palsy or polio, not realizing that people with disabilities are in control of their lives and rarely in constant pain.

There are some subtler ways in which language stigmatizes people with disabilities. For example, referring to someone who is disabled as "a handicapped" person does two things: 1) it perpetuates the use of the word handicapped which, although it is widely used by the federal government, the medical profession, and the general public, conveys a sense of neediness and dependence that disability rights activists have been working hard to dispel; and 2) it continues to make the "handicap" the factor of prime importance about the person. Using instead an expression such as "a person who is disabled" or "a person who is blind," conveys that the disability is only one trait of that person. Such differences in expression might seem subtle or even unimportant to someone who hasn't thought about the issue before. When one considers, however, that language is a primary means of communicating attitudes, thoughts, and feelings to young children, the elimination of words and expressions that stereotype becomes an essential part of creating an inclusive environment.

INCORPORATING DISABILITY AWARENESS INTO THE CURRICULUM

As the curricular activities described in this guide make clear, an in-clusive approach can be integrated into the standard early childhood curriculum. For example, the concept of same and different is a natural vehicle for learning about hearing, visual, and mobility impairments and for what is the same and different in all of us. When studying the human body in a body parts curriculum unit, children readily accept that people with disabilities may use certain parts of their bodies or move differently than nondisabled people. Children also learn that some people with disabilities adapt, use aids, and often can do the same activities, albeit differently, as nondisabled people. Transporta-tion, another standard unit in the early childhood curriculum, extends the usual exploration of how nondisabled people move from place to place—by creeping (when they were babies), by walking, and by using wheeled vehicles such as wagons, cars, and buses—to include some of the ways that people with mobility impairments move from place to place—by using crutches, braces, walkers, scooterboards, and wheel-chairs. This expanded unit also leads to the beginnings of a social con-sciousness about the importance of an accessible environment.

In short, including a disability focus in the everyday life of the classroom builds upon and enhances the regular curriculum, regard-less of whether the program is mainstreamed, nonmainstreamed, or special education. Children who participated in the pilot testing of Pro-ject Inclusive were intensely interested in learning about various disabil-ities. These children explored and examined their school environment in new ways: they met women and men with disabilities who became role models; they brought information home to their families, which in-creased parent/child and home/school communication; and they learned some words in American Sign Language, which allowed them to communicate in a new way while improving their small motor coor-dination.

The cognitive skills gained from participating in the pilot test, which was very brief, far exceeded anyone's expectations. For example, before the start of the project, children in the three-, four-, and five-year-old classes were interviewed to find out what they knew about disabilities. The three- and four-year-olds did not have very accurate perceptions, e.g., one child said that "blind means you are dead" and another thought that being deaf meant that "you were a big girl." These younger children, although quite familiar with Linda Bove on *Sesame Street,* did not understand that she is deaf, even though they all knew that she spoke in sign language. The five-year-olds showed considerably more knowledge during their pretest interviews. At least half of them said they knew someone who was blind or deaf, and many of them mentioned Linda Bove.

At the end of the pilot-testing period, the differences between the three age groups had lessened considerably. *All* the children understood what it meant to be blind and to be deaf, and children from *every* group talked about people they knew personally who were disabled. One important gain was that the five-year-olds demonstrated increased sensitivity about disability bias. Before the pilot testing, some of the five-year-olds had called each other "blind" to tease or insult. By the end of the project, when one child began to make such a comment, two others quickly intervened saying, "It is not funny." The first child became defensive and explained, "I was only going to say being blind means you can't see." After exposure to actual role models, the five-year-olds also changed their comments about disability from what a person couldn't do, e.g., "People who are blind can't drive," to a more positive view, e.g., "People who are blind can swim."

Learning American Sign Language proved to be a cognitive and social learning experience for children, teachers, and parents. Everyone started out at the same level, knowing no signs, and was able to progress at her or his own pace. Some of the children who were not verbally articulate were intrigued and challenged by learning signs. Children problem-solved as they figured out the pictures in the sign language books, they helped each other to learn new signs, and they taught signs to children in other classes. They also taught their teachers and parents new signs. One child learned to sign her mother's first name as a surprise and, at a parent meeting, a mother reported with delight that her child had begun to communicate for the first time with a 17-year-old neighbor who is deaf. One teacher's comment really sums it up—"Not only did the children learn new skills, like signing, they became more aware of other children's feelings."

All the cognitive, social, emotional, and physical skills that an inclusive curriculum fosters are gained through hands-on, experiential activities that are in keeping with the natural learning style of children and are comfortable for teachers. Girls and boys participate equally in all the activities. Activities can involve learning to walk with crutches or interacting with a child-size doll outfitted with a battery-pack hearing aid worn in a chest harness. No activity is superimposed—each one grows out of a curriculum already in effect. From the activities, however, the children gain new knowledge, skills, and insights. They learn that disability is a part of life and that people with disabilities can do many things in many different ways. Children learn to accept differences, and they learn from and with people who are disabled. Above all, whether disabled themselves or not, they learn to be comfortable with disability—something that most people have never had the opportunity to learn.

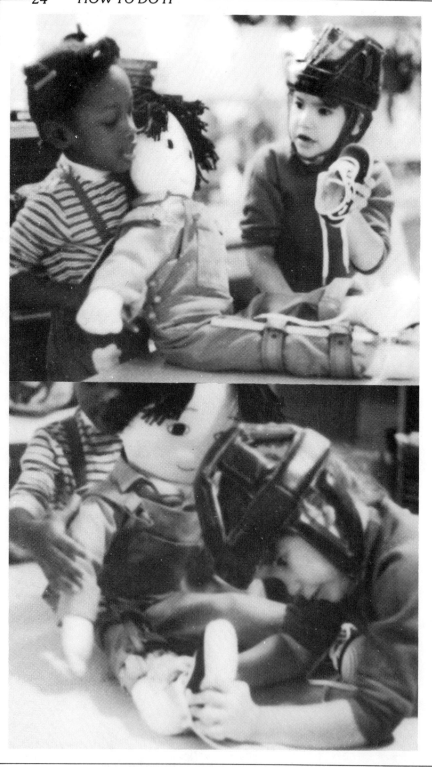

The Inclusive Curriculum: How To Do It

An inclusive curriculum—one that is nonsexist, multicultural, and includes images of children and adults with disabilities—can be integrated naturally into the standard early childhood curriculum. This guide tells how to do it and focuses on three traditional preschool units: Same/Different, Body Parts, and Transportation. Each unit incorporates one disability: hearing impairment in Same/Different, visual impairment in Body Parts, and mobility impairment in Transportation.

Each unit contains an overview, a preliminary activity, and six sequential activities. The overview highlights how learning about disability builds upon and extends good early childhood practices. The overview also contains a list of the activities as well as the materials used in that unit.

Following the overview is a preliminary activity that sets the stage for the ensuing curriculum. For example, "Individual Differences" introduces the concept of same/different in a positive way; "Learning About Our Bodies" presents basic information about body parts, and "Making Footprints" helps children understand the beginning of independent mobility and transportation. In addition to the preliminary activity, each unit contains six step-by-step activities, which are organized into the following sections: Purposes, What Children Learn, Format, Materials and Supplies, Background Information, Activity, Equity Issues, Be Aware, and Alternatives. The Background Information section relates information about the disability that is relevant to the specific activity. The Equity Issues section calls attention to ways to redress sex, race, and disability stereotyping. The Be Aware section points out any other general pitfalls that the teacher needs to watch out for. Everything is based on first-hand experiences from the Project Inclusive pilot testing.

While each curriculum area focuses on a specific disability, many of the activities can cross over among units. For example, learning about hearing impairment is as relevant to the Body Parts unit as to the unit on Same/Different, learning about visual impairment is as relevant to the Transportation unit as it is to the unit on Body Parts, and mobility impairment is as relevant to a Same/Different unit as it is to the unit on Transportation.

Within the unit, the activities are sequential, each building upon children's previous learning. The units can be used separately, and the activities should become an ongoing part of the life of the classroom. Together, the units provide a curriculum that reflects the reality and needs of all children. While the activities have been written with an easy-to-use, step-by-step approach, they are not meant to be used as "cookbook" recipes. Every classroom situation is unique, every teacher's style of teaching is different, and every child's learning mode is entirely her or his own. Read through all the activities before you begin to use them. The curriculum will be most effective if you make it your own, adapting it to the particular needs of the children in your classroom.

ROLE MODELS

As with all good early childhood teaching, children learn best from real life experiences. Introducing a person with a disability into the daily life of the classroom provides unparalleled learning opportunities. This was proven dramatically during the pilot testing of Project Inclusive through the interaction of the children with Ellen Rubin, a project staff member who is blind. It may be possible to recruit a volunteer who is disabled to work with you in your classroom on an ongoing basis.

Inviting people with disabilities to visit the classroom also provides excellent opportunities for learning. For example, as part of the Same/Different curriculum, you can invite a sign language interpreter and a person with a hearing impairment who uses sign language to visit your class. Or, as happened during the pilot testing, you can invite a person who uses a guide dog to visit as an extension of the Body Parts or Transportation curriculum.

Before any visitor comes to the classroom, it is a good idea to prepare both the children for the visitor and the visitor for the children's questions. Not everyone is accustomed to answering the direct questions of three-, four-, and five-year-olds in an appropriate manner. It is important to make sure that whoever you invite be comfortable and open enough to discuss her or his disability in a manner that is appropriate to the age level of the children in your class. It is also important that she or he be aware of what has been taking place in your classroom to be able to support your efforts. You may find visitors who fit these criteria by contacting a community office for the disabled or an activist consumer group. You will find additional suggestions in the Resources section at the end of the guide. Ask the people you invite to talk about their work and any special talents they have as well as issues related to their disability.

COMMUNITY EXTENSIONS

Learning about disability can provide opportunities for involving the larger school community. For example, ask a parent or a staff member who is handy at carpentry to make a wheelchair scaled for use in the block corner. Or have children take trips around the school and the neighboring community to look at them in terms of accessibility, e.g., are there curb cuts? special parking places? ramps? elevators with Braille buttons?

During the pilot testing of the Transportation unit, a person who did woodworking with the children turned a wagon into a wheelchair. The teacher then arranged for a visit from a ramp-equipped school bus that transports children who are mobility impaired. The bus driver explained to the class how the bus worked, and all the children had a chance to walk up the ramp, to push their wagon-turned-wheelchair, and to look inside the bus. The visit was so successful that the bus and driver returned a second time so other classrooms could see it. During this trip, children from the first class helped to describe the bus to the other children.

ANSWERING CHILDREN'S QUESTIONS

Children ask many questions regarding their environment and the people and things in it. Questions about disability will be no exception. Basic rules for answering questions related to disability and the equipment and devices used by people with disabilities are really the same as for answering all children's questions:

- Answer as honestly as you can. If you do not know the answer, perhaps you, together with the child, can look for the answer in an appropriate book or other resource.

- Keep it simple. Do not burden young children with lengthy complicated information when a clear statement will do.

- Use accurate terminology, even if the words seem long and unfamiliar, e.g., disability and accessibility. Children love learning new and "fancy" words, and it is important that a child begin to use the correct words.

- Be sensitive to what the child is "really" asking. Sometimes children want information, but sometimes they want to know, "What does this mean for me?"

- Be nonjudgmental in your approach.

As with sex and race, disability bias in language is also pervasive. It is necessary to choose words carefully and to listen to words children use as clues to their attitudes. (See discussion of language bias in the Introduction.)

"NEW FRIEND" DOLLS

As will become apparent as you read the three curriculum units, a resource called "New Friends" plays an important role in the inclusive activities. "New Friends" are dolls that are part of an extensive program developed by the Chapel Hill Training Outreach Project (see Resources section). Approximately the size of a three-year-old, the dolls are made from an easy-to-follow, do-it-yourself pattern that comes with various suggestions for adapting the doll to represent someone with a disability. A talented staff member or a family member of one of the children could be enlisted to help with making the dolls at your center.

The dolls help to introduce a disability to children and provide excellent opportunities for children to ask questions. As the dolls become a permanent part of the classroom, they help children become comfortable with the concept of disability and become familiar with various pieces of adaptive equipment. In addition, the dolls also provide an opportunity to talk about various cultures. The three dolls that were made for the pilot testing of Project Inclusive were multiracial: Black,

Asian, and Caucasian. The children responded to the ethnicity of the dolls, thus providing the teacher with a further opportunity for discussion.

Since the dolls provide such good learning opportunities, it is strongly suggested that you have them made for use at your center. If you are making more than one doll, be sure they provide a multiracial component to the curriculum. The dolls could be made to reflect the cultural variety of the children in your class or, in the case of a homogeneous class, they could provide the opportunity to introduce a pluralistic view of the world. In making the dolls, however, it is necessary to watch out for potential stereotyping in the racial or ethnic characteristic of the doll, e.g., if the doll is to be Asian, the skin should not be bright yellow, and almond-shaped eyes are much more realistic than the racist stereotype of "slanty" eyes.

Also, as is discussed in the curriculum activities, androgynous-looking dolls provide wider opportunities for imaginative play and do not predetermine children's choice of name for their playmate. Short hair cuts and play clothes appropriate for boys and girls, e.g., overalls and T-shirt, will help make the doll anything the children want it to be.

If it is only possible to make one doll, do not change the disability of the doll to fit the appropriate unit, i.e., the doll should not be hearing impaired one month, mobility impaired the next. This would be contrary to the reality that you are trying to present to children about people with disabilities, and it certainly would give false messages about the permanent nature of most disabilities.

CREATING AN INCLUSIVE ENVIRONMENT FOR ALL CHILDREN

By using the materials and activities in this guide, nonstereotyped images of children and adults, disabled and nondisabled, will be integrated into the daily life of the classroom. The guide contains an early childhood curriculum about disability. It does not, however, contain the information to adapt your classroom to the specific needs of every child with a disability. For this, you will have to keep an open mind, looking for new ways of approaching each situation, using and extending the ideas in this guide for each child. In addition the Annotated Bibliography at the end of the guide provides information about a wealth of resources that you can tap for help in about every situation.

This guide asks you to think of new ways to approach ongoing teaching situations, particularly in regard to issues of sex, race, and disability. By making the classroom nonsexist, multicultural, and accessible to children with disabilities, you will be making the classroom a better place for all children. Through this effort, the early childhood environment truly will be including all of us.

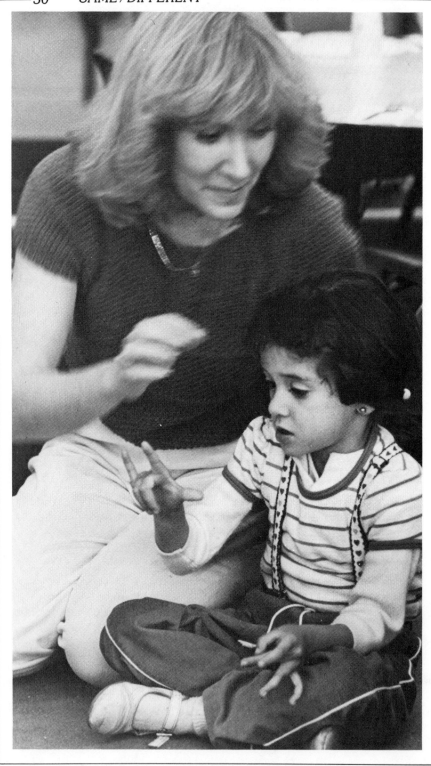

Same/Different

OVERVIEW

Learning about disability adds a new dimension to the traditional same/different early childhood curriculum. In addition to learning what is same and different in terms of comparisons in the physical environment, children examine what is the same and what is different about themselves in relation to others.

The activities that follow extend a same/different curriculum to include the concept of hearing impairment. They help children to understand that a person who is hearing impaired may be different from them in one respect, but similar in many others. By recognizing the differences, but focusing on the similarities, children come to accept people for who they are.

One advantage of this focus is that it helps to draw out children's sensitivity to each other. For example, in one class during the pilot testing, Janelle, a three-year-old girl, was having difficulty adjusting, and teachers were beginning to think it was because of a sporadic hearing impairment. As a result, Janelle was going through a series of outside tests. Even though this had not been discussed in the classroom, Kareem, a four-year-old boy, went over to Janelle, handed her a paper ear trumpet, and said, "Here, Janelle, use this, it will help you to hear." Janelle put it to her ear, listened, and just smiled.

The activities that follow also use the concept of hearing impairment as a jumping off point to teach children some words in American Sign Language (ASL). Learning sign language can become a focal point of the curriculum and can extend far beyond the classroom walls. During the pilot testing, children were so fascinated with this new form of communication that they couldn't learn it fast enough. They learned new signs from books placed in the classroom. They informally taught each other new signs and then were invited to other classrooms as "teachers." They also taught their own teachers new signs and went home and taught their parents as well.

The Same/Different curriculum activities include:

PRELIMINARY
ACTIVITY   *Individual Differences*

ACTIVITY I   *Introducing a "New Friend" and the Concept of Hearing Impairment*

ACTIVITY II   *One Difference and Many Similarities*

ACTIVITY III   *American Sign Language (ASL): I Love You*

ACTIVITY IV   *American Sign Language (ASL): Expressing Feelings*

ACTIVITY V   *American Sign Language (ASL): From Good Morning to Good Night*

ACTIVITY VI   *Children Teaching Children*

Materials

Battery-Pack Hearing Aids. Local hearing aid dealers may be a source.

Linda Bove, Actress (poster). TABS: Aids for Ending Sexism in School, 744 Carroll St., Brooklyn, NY 11215.

"New Friend" doll (pattern). The Chapel Hill Training Outreach Project, Lincoln Center, Merritt Hill Rd., Chapel Hill, NC 27514.

Sesame Street Sign Language Fun (book). New York: Random House /Children's Television Workshop, 1980.

Who Am I? (book). Northbrook, IL: Hubbard, 1975.

Why Am I Different? (book). Chicago: Albert Whitman & Co., 1976.

Alternative Materials

A Button in Her Ear (book). Chicago: Albert Whitman & Co., 1976.

Handmade ABC: Manual Alphabet (book). Reading, MA: Addison, Wesley, 1981.

I Have a Sister, My Sister Is Deaf (book). New York: Harper and Row, 1977.

National Association for the Deaf Bookstore. 814 Thayer Ave., Silver Springs, MD 20910.

Resource Photos for Mainstreaming: Children Set. Women's Action Alliance, Inc., 370 Lexington Ave., New York, NY 10017.

PRELIMINARY ACTIVITY

Individual Differences

PURPOSES

- To introduce the concept of human differences in a positive way.
- To help children begin to understand the origins of difference, e.g., growth and development, heredity, personal preference, life-style.
- To help children accept their human differences as part of a positive self-image.

WHAT CHILDREN LEARN

- To view differences positively.
- The concept of same/different through comparison.
- That human differences make the world more varied and interesting.

FORMAT

A. Large-group circle time for reading book (15 minutes).
B. Follow-up charting activities (10 minutes per activity).

MATERIALS AND SUPPLIES

Why Am I Different?
This nonsexist, multicultural book celebrates human differences. Children will recognize themselves in the illustrations of school, family,

and play scenes. Older people are depicted as active, and urban and suburban settings are represented.

Paper and magic markers

ACTIVITY

A. *Large-group circle time*

During circle time read the book *Why Am I Different?*. Have a discussion about the ways children in the class are alike and different. Following the discussion, pick one area of difference, e.g., hair color, (how many children have brown hair, black hair, red hair, blonde hair?) and make a class chart about it.

B. *Follow-up charting activity*

On subsequent days, continue to discuss and make charts about differences, e.g., eye color, favorite foods, languages spoken by the children, favorite activities, places children live (house, apartment, trailer, boat). For some of the charts, you may want to cut out pictures to represent objects.

EQUITY ISSUES

The illustrations in *Why Am I Different?* are multicultural and, with one exception, nonsexist. (One of the first differences depicted is size, and it is illustrated with a tall boy and a small girl, one of the most common sex stereotypes.) The book does not, however, include any children or adults with disabilities. Despite this lack of inclusion, the perspective on human differences throughout is positive, and the book can be used as an introduction to the same/different curriculum.

BE AWARE

During class discussions, be careful not to have children make value judgments on differences such as size. Focus the discussion on how, while human beings have many differences, there are many more traits that we all share. Because the illustrations in *Why Am I Different?* are mostly in black and white, it is sometimes difficult to see differences such as hair color.

ALTERNATIVES

If the book *Why Am I Different?* is not available, the charting activities can stand on their own and should be used as an introduction to the concept of same/different.

ACTIVITY I

Introducing a "New Friend" and the Concept of Hearing Impairment

PURPOSES

- To introduce the concept of hearing impairment.
- To help children understand that people hear differently.
- To introduce the concept of amplification.
- To introduce new vocabulary related to hearing impairment.
- To relate hearing impairment to the children's own experiences, e.g., family members, classmates, teachers.

WHAT CHILDREN LEARN

- That there are different degrees of hearing ability.
- That a hearing aid can help some people to hear better.
- That there are different ways to amplify sound.
- New vocabulary related to hearing impairment, e.g., disability, hearing aid, battery pack, amplify.

FORMAT

A. Large-group circle time for introduction of doll (15 minutes).
B. Small groups for loud/soft sounds follow-up (10-20 minutes per group).

MATERIALS AND SUPPLIES

"New Friend" doll with a battery-pack hearing aid in a harness

This doll, which is made from a do-it-yourself pattern, is about the size of a three-year-old and can become very "realistic" to the children. The pattern for the doll comes with suggestions for making a representation of a harness for a battery-pack hearing aid. You also can make your own. Project Inclusive, for example, made the harness straps from one-inch wide white elastic, and the pocket to hold the battery

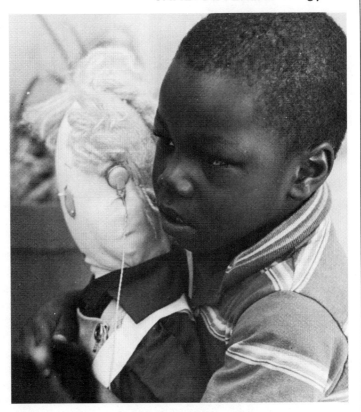

pack was made from a toe cut off a white sock. The pieces were held together by Velcro so the harness could be taken on and off easily. So it can be removed, the hearing aid should be attached to the doll's "ear" with Velcro. If possible, a bilateral hearing aid should be used, since it is the type frequently used by young children.

Radio, or cassette player and tape, or record player and record

Ear muffs

Paper ear trumpet
The trumpet can be made from construction paper or oaktag, approximately $12'' \times 20''$.

BACKGROUND INFORMATION

A hearing aid helps amplify sounds. Most hearing aids are small and fit in or around a person's ear(s). Others are attached by a cord to a battery pack that fits in a pocket or, for a young child, on a special harness on the chest or back. Some people wear a hearing aid in both ears. This is called a bilateral or bineural hearing aid. For information about hearing impairment, which will help to answer children's questions, see Resources section.

ACTIVITY

A. *Large-group circle time*

1 . Introduce the "New Friend" doll to the children during circle time; most likely children will want to give the doll a name.

2 . Ask children to tell anything that they notice about the doll. Children may talk about doll's clothing, hair, "skin" color, and so forth, without mentioning the battery-pack hearing aid. If they do notice the hearing aid, they may not know what it is. Some children might think the hearing aid is a microphone, or a portable radio, or a hiking pack. Be sure to allow children time to explore all possibilities.

3 . If children cannot identify the hearing aid, help them by pointing out that the pack is attached by cord to the doll's "ear." (It was at this point in the pilot test that the children made the connection that the pack helped the doll to hear.) Be sure that before the discussion is over children receive accurate information: that the doll is wearing a hearing aid and that the purpose of a hearing aid is to make louder the sounds one hears. Point out that a hearing aid helps people to hear better, the way glasses help people to see better.

4 . Ask children if they know anyone who uses a hearing aid. There may be children in the class, a teacher, or a relative. If there is a child in the class who uses a hearing aid, check beforehand to see if she or he would be willing to talk about it. How does the hearing aid work? Why does she or he need it?

5 . After discussion is completed, put the new doll into the dramatic play or other appropriate classroom area, where she or he will become a permanent part of the classroom scene.

B. *Loud/soft sounds small-group follow-up*

1 . Work with children in pairs over a number of days until all have had the opportunity to participate. Have them experiment with loud and soft sounds. Play a record (or radio or tape) at different sound levels. Have children experiment listening to the loud music with their hands over both their ears, over one ear at a time, and wearing ear muffs.

2 . Have children listen to soft music and then use the paper ear trumpet. What happens? Have children use the ear trumpet to listen to other sounds, e.g., children talking in the classroom, the sound of rain on the window. Have children talk softly into

the ear trumpet, treating it like a megaphone. What happens to the sound of their voices?

3 . At this point, the connection should be made between the different ways the children have been hearing sounds and the different way people who are hearing impaired hear sounds. Also, they should realize that a hearing aid helps to make sounds louder for people with hearing impairments.

4 . If you are able to obtain a working hearing aid, now is the time to demonstrate to children how it is used. First, test the volume of the hearing aid to make sure it is not too loud. Then, while children hold ear attachment to their ears, either talk softly into the battery pack, or tap it with a pencil, or have children listen to the record again. If children are going to speak into the battery pack, caution them to speak very softly so as not to hurt the ear of the child who is listening.

EQUITY ISSUES

For a full discussion of the equity issues involved in making a "New Friend" doll, see The Inclusive Curriculum: How To Do It. For example, it is important to dress the doll in typical play clothes suitable for both sexes, i.e., overalls and T-shirt; to give the doll a hairdo that is not obviously for a girl or a boy; to be sensitive to potential stereotyping in the ethnicity of the doll. Also, do not refer to the doll as "she" or "he" in advance, thus influencing the children's choice of name for the doll.

BE AWARE

It is important to supervise very closely children's use of a working hearing aid. It will emit a high piercing squeal or feedback when the ear mold fits poorly or if the volume is too high. When not in supervised use, it is a good idea to remove the batteries from the hearing aid. Also, for safety and for health reasons the paper ear trumpet should be made to fit *around* an ear.

ALTERNATIVES

A stethoscope also can be used to demonstrate how sounds are made louder. As with the hearing aid, children should be cautioned to speak into the stethoscope very softly so as not to hurt the ear of the child who is listening. If it is not possible to make a "New Friend" doll, a battery-pack hearing aid in a harness could be made to fit one of the existing dolls in the classroom.

ACTIVITY II

One Difference and Many Similarities

PURPOSES

- To help hearing and hearing-impaired children understand the many similarities among themselves.
- To reinforce children's knowledge about hearing impairment and hearing aids.
- To provide a positive role model of a child with a disability.
- To provide a catalyst for children to discuss emotions.
- To reinforce children's knowledge about hearing impairment and hearing aids.

WHAT CHILDREN LEARN

- That all children, disabled and nondisabled, share a variety of emotions.
- To articulate their own feelings and emotions.
- That all children, disabled and nondisabled, do many of the same things.
- To observe and discuss the physical similarities and differences between themselves and the girl in the book *Who Am I?*
- Information that reinforces their prior knowledge about hearing impairment.
- Listening and discussion skills.

FORMAT

A. Large-group circle time for reading of book (15 minutes).

B. Small groups for drawing as part of choices during free play (15-30 minutes).

MATERIALS AND SUPPLIES

Who Am I?

Children will identify with the wonderful nonstereotypical photographs in this book about a young Black girl and her family. It shows her playing with friends, loving various family members, and expressing a wide range of emotions. The title words, "Who Am I?" are the only words that appear periodically throughout the book, until the end, when the girl answers, "Me!" The main character wears a battery-pack hearing aid in a harness, like the one the class's new doll wears (see Activity I).

Art Materials
Paper and crayons, magic markers, or paint.

BACKGROUND INFORMATION

For information on the purpose of hearing aids and the different kinds available, see Background Information in Activity I.

ACTIVITY

A. *Large-group circle time*

1. Read *Who Am I?* to the class. Since there are few words in the book, the pictures should be used to ask children: What is happening? What is the girl doing? Have you ever done that? How does the girl in the picture feel? When do you feel that way?

2. If, by the end of the story, the children have not noticed that the girl is wearing a hearing aid, ask them if there is anything that is the same about the girl in the story and the new doll in the classroom. Talk again about how the hearing aid helps the girl to hear better. Chances are, however, that the children will notice the hearing aid on their own. During the pilot testing, for example, one of the children commented after a few pages, "She has a hearing aid in her ear." The teacher asked, "Do we know someone else who wears a hearing aid?" And the children all responded, "Judy!" (their new doll). When the teacher wondered, "Why is she wearing a hearing aid?" The children answered, "To help her hear better."

3. During the discussion of the book, it is important to emphasize the *similarities* between the girl in the book and the children in your class. There may be one difference, e.g., the fact that she is hearing-impaired, but there are many similarities.

4. After reading and discussing *Who Am I?*, the book should become a permanent part of the classroom library.

B. *Small-group drawing*

As one of the choices during free play, have the children do drawing as a follow-up to reading *Who Am I?* While not pressured to do representational art, during the pilot testing the children drew pictures of their favorite scenes in the book. Several children drew amazingly accurate representations of the hearing aid as well.

Older children could be asked to draw pictures of "who I am." Pictures should then be put up around the room.

EQUITY ISSUES

The book *Who Am I?* is an excellent inclusive resource because: a) It does not make the main character's disability the focus of the story; b) It depicts a Black family; c) The main character is an active girl with both female and male friends; d) Males and females are shown as caregivers; e) It portrays a positive view of older adults; and f) It shows children expressing a wide range of emotions. These are characteristics worth having in every book.

BE AWARE

It is possible, since children are so literal, that they will think the girl in the book is asking, "Who Am I?" because she doesn't know her name. (Several of the younger children did think this during the pilot testing.) You may need to help children to move beyond this literal interpretation by focusing on the girl's emotions and questioning attitudes.

ALTERNATIVES

To make the classroom more inclusive, it would be a good idea to hang photographs of children and adults who are hearing impaired at children's eye level in the dramatic play area or book corner to encourage child-to-child or teacher-to-child discussion. It is important to try to have a balance of age, gender, and race/ethnicity in the pictures and to have them reflect what is happening in the classroom. The children's set of *Resource Photos for Mainstreaming* contains two excellent photographs of children wearing battery-pack hearing aids in a harness that is similar to the one worn by the girl in *Who Am I?* It is also possible to take photographs of children in the class or to clip out interactive, positive pictures from brochures, journals, or magazines put out by consumer groups, educational organizations, or hearing-aid distributors. For older children, the books *A Button in Her Ear* and *I Have a Sister, My Sister Is Deaf* would make good additions to the classroom library.

Overheard in book corner while children are discussing *Who Am I?*: "Her hair is just like mine." "You're white; she's brown, like me." "I .have a grandfather, too." "She looks angry." "There's her hearing aid again."

ACTIVITY III

American Sign Language (ASL):
I Love You

PURPOSES

- To expand the concept of communication to include American Sign Language (ASL).
- To teach children to say "I love you" in ASL and other languages such as Spanish, French, and Cantonese.
- To reinforce vocabulary development.

WHAT CHILDREN LEARN

- New vocabulary and information related to hearing impairment, e.g., American Sign Language.
- That ASL is one language of many used to communicate.
- How to say "I love you" in several languages including ASL.

FORMAT

Large-group circle time (15-20 minutes).

MATERIALS AND SUPPLIES

Linda Bove, Actress
A poster featuring Linda Bove, a regular cast member of *Sesame Street*, signing "I love you." (The poster caption interprets the sign more broadly to mean "I like you.")
Strips of paper and markers

BACKGROUND INFORMATION

The poster comes with a short biography of Linda Bove, entitled "Breaking Down Barriers," which discusses her growing up, education, and work. Linda Bove, a member of the National Theatre of the Deaf, uses ASL to communicate. For a fuller description of different means of communication used by people who are hearing impaired, see Resources section.

ACTIVITY

1. Put up the Linda Bove poster at children's eye level near the circle-activity area of the room.

2. During circle time, ask children if they watch *Sesame Street*. Do they know Linda? Ask them to tell you anything they remember about Linda. How does Linda talk? Does she use sign language? Ask children why Linda uses sign language. Explain that Linda is deaf. Linda communicates with people by using American Sign Language because she cannot hear the words people say. Do children know anyone besides Linda who uses sign language?

3. Point out the poster and give children a chance to take a close look at it. The main photograph on the poster is of Linda signing "I love you." Have children make the same sign. If there are children who are hearing impaired in the class who use sign language, and if

they agree, involve them in this activity. Have them help you teach sign language throughout the curriculum.

4. Ask children how else they can let someone know they love them, e.g., a smile, a hug, a happy face. Do they always use words to let people know how they feel?

5. Talk about how there are many ways to communicate. Do any children in the class know another language? Do they know anyone who speaks another language? Depending on the ethnic make up of the class, have a list ready of how to say "I love you" in many languages (see examples at end of this unit).

6. Write "I love you" in different languages on strips of paper and put them near the Linda Bove poster.

7. Use the sign for "I love you" as many times during the day as possible. It will be just the beginning of its use throughout the year!

EQUITY ISSUES

Children, for a variety of reasons, come to early childhood classrooms with varying vocabularies. When learning words in American Sign Language, however, all hearing children start at the same level. Sign language fosters language development for all children. Children who are able to sign easily will help those who have more difficulty. Some children might participate more fully than they had previously. Teaching new words in a variety of languages validates each one. It will help to counteract the attitude that English is the only "good" language.

BE AWARE

It's important to watch out for confusion on the children's part about why a person uses sign language. Children may think that a person uses sign language because she or he can't talk. Hearing and speech impairments sometimes, though not always, do go together. When working with young children, it is not necessary to go into great detail. But if the confusion arises, it is important to let them know that American Sign Language is used not because people can't talk, but because they cannot hear the words other people say.

ALTERNATIVES

If a home activity is possible, ask children to watch _Sesame Street_— after school, during vacation, on the weekend—and to look for Linda. Then talk in class about what they saw. This activity can take place just as effectively before or after the poster is introduced and the children learn the "I love you" sign.

ACTIVITY IV

A four-year-old boy went to the book corner and selected *The Little Engine That Could.* When he got to the page where the little engine and toys were happy, he made the sign for happy. He also made the sign for sad when the engine was sad.

American Sign Language (ASL): Expressing Feelings

PURPOSES

- To help children discuss their feelings and to explore the many ways they express them.
- To help children review and expand their ASL vocabulary.

WHAT CHILDREN LEARN

- That it is important for everyone to be able to express her or his feelings.
- That each person needs to be aware of how other people are feeling.
- That there are different ways to communicate feelings.
- How to say "happy," "sad," "angry," and "surprised" in ASL.

FORMAT

Large-group circle time (20 minutes).

MATERIALS AND SUPPLIES

Sesame Street Sign Language Fun
A colorful, simple sign language book in which Linda Bove illustrates the signs for words and expressions familiar to preschoolers.

Who Am I?
See Activity II for a description of this book.

BACKGROUND INFORMATION

How to say "happy," "sad," "angry," and "surprised" in American Sign Language as well as other languages can be found at the end of this unit. When demonstrating the signs, it is important to have your facial expression reflect the same feeling, e.g., smiling when happy, frowning when angry.

ACTIVITY

1. During circle time, reread *Who Am I?* focusing on how the little girl is feeling. Have children talk about the times when they have felt happy or sad or angry or surprised.

2. Ask children how they look when they are happy, angry, sad, or surprised. How do they let people know how they are feeling? Facial expressions? Body language? Words?

3. Ask children if they remember how to say "I love you" in American Sign Language. Have them practice the sign again.

4. Ask children how they think one would say "happy," "sad," "angry," and "surprised" in American Sign Language. Children can have fun making up their own signs. Then, show them the American Sign Language in the *Sesame Street Sign Language Fun* book. Help children make the proper signs and practice with them.

5. Put *Sign Language Fun* in the book corner or in a special place of its own. It is important that children be able to go to it when they are interested. You will find that children will use the book as a reference so that they can teach themselves new signs.

6. Consider making a sign language corner, putting the book near the Linda Bove poster. Put the new words that children learn on strips of paper and mount them on a wall or bulletin board near the poster.

EQUITY ISSUES

It is important to help all children express a full range of emotions. Given the "boys don't cry" and "take it like a man" stereotypes that still pervade our culture, it is especially important to let little boys know that it is all right to have feelings and that expressing them is important, too.

Most of the illustrations in the *Sign Language Fun* book are non-sexist. However, the authors slipped up in their use of "policeman" in the People in the Neighborhood section. This can be corrected simply by covering the word with white tape and replacing it with the more inclusive term, police officer. This could be a good discussion stimulator about language for the children and other teachers as well.

BE AWARE

You may need to help children understand that American Sign Language is a language, like any other language. It is important that children not think it is simply a series of gestures and facial expressions.

ALTERNATIVES

If the *Sign Language Fun* book is not available, it is important to find some appropriate sign language resource for children to use. The National Association for the Deaf has a bookstore where alternative possibilities are available. It is possible that books on ASL are available from the local library or a bookstore. You could use the book to copy the appropriate signs and make your own classroom book of signs. Glue a different sign to each page; children may want to draw pictures to go with the signs.

If possible, continue to provide different language translations for each new word learned in American Sign Language (see chart at end of this unit).

ACTIVITY V

American Sign Language (ASL): From Good Morning to Good Night

PURPOSES

- To incorporate American Sign Language into the everyday life of the classroom.
- To review with children the signs that they have already learned.
- To teach children ASL for "good morning," "good night," and other familiar words and phrases.

WHAT CHILDREN LEARN

- To accept and use American Sign Language as a regular means of communication.
- Problem-solving and decoding skills as they teach themselves new signs.
- Reading skills as they recognize signs around the room, in books, on the bulletin board.

FORMAT

Large-group circle time (15-30 minutes).

MATERIALS AND SUPPLIES

Sesame Street Sign Language Fun
See Activity IV for a description of the book.

ACTIVITY

1. Review signs children have learned: I love you, happy, sad, angry, surprised.

2. Ask children how they think you would say "good morning" and "good night" in ASL.

3. Show children the signs for "good morning" and "good night" and have them practice.

4. Use the good morning sign every day when greeting children and the good night sign when they go home at the end of the day.

5. Add words to American Sign Language bulletin board.

EQUITY ISSUES

See previous activities (III, IV) about American Sign Language.

BE AWARE

See previous activities (III, IV) about American Sign Language.

ALTERNATIVES

The possibilities for expanding children's experience through learning different words in ASL are endless. Children could learn the signs for the day's weather, or the days of the week, or for Happy Birthday. During the pilot testing, for example, at the end of just four weeks, the children's "Sign Language Words We Know" bulletin board had expanded to include: I like you, happy, sad, angry, good morning, good night, grow, butterfly, cookie, mother, father, grandfather, grandmother, baby, sister, brother, stand, sit, kneel, walk, run, climb, and the sentence, "I want to read a book about cookies."

Other children might be interested in the manual alphabet (finger spelling). One resource is *Handmade ABC: Manual Alphabet*, a book illustrating each letter of the alphabet with an appropriate drawing and the finger sign. To finger spell their names, children need to know only the first letter of their name; then they "place" that letter somewhere on their bodies, e.g., over their heart, their lips, their shoulder. If children have their names written out in the classroom—on their cubbies, for example—they also can match the finger spelling sign to each letter of their names.

ACTIVITY VI

Children Teaching Children

PURPOSES

- To extend American Sign Language communication to other classrooms.
- To have children experience the role of teacher.

WHAT CHILDREN LEARN

- Planning skills as they prepare to visit other classrooms.
- How to share skills and knowledge with others.
- What it feels like to be a teacher.

FORMAT

Visiting another class's large-group circle time (15 minutes).

MATERIALS AND SUPPLIES

None.

BACKGROUND INFORMATION

See previous American Sign Language activities (III, IV, V).

ACTIVITY

1. Arrange in advance with another teacher for two or three children to visit her or his classroom during circle time. If possible, select a class whose children are the same age as those in your class.

2. Explain to your children that they are going to visit another class and teach the children there some words in American Sign Language. Ask for volunteers, and if there are too many, select three children and assure the others that they will have a chance to go at a later date.

3. Have children visit other classes and teach them how to sign, "I love you." It might be a good idea for the children to take the Linda Bove poster with them, so they can talk about seeing her on *Sesame Street*.

4. On follow-up visits, have other children visit the class and teach different signs.

EQUITY ISSUES

In selecting groups of children to go to teach in other classrooms, be sure to have a mix of girls and boys. Select groups in such a way that one child will not take over and dominate.

BE AWARE

It is necessary to spend some time preparing the children to be "teachers." Children may be so excited about their own knowledge of sign language that they will want to show off all the words they know at once to the other class. Remind the children that they learned one word at a time; explain that one has to teach a new idea slowly. It also would be a good idea to reverse roles and practice with the children beforehand, letting them be the teachers and you the student.

ALTERNATIVES

Another way to help children feel comfortable teaching in another classroom is for them to bring the "New Friend" doll for a visit. They could introduce her or him to the new class and explain about the battery-pack hearing aid. They could teach the "I love you" sign during the same session. A second group of children could go to the class a few days later, pick up the doll, and teach "good morning" and "good night." This also is an effective way to begin to create an inclusive environment throughout the center or school.

If you have been learning new words in other languages as well as American Sign Language, children could teach other children all the new ways they have learned to communicate.

LEARNING WORDS IN MANY LANGUAGES

Included on the chart that follows are those signs that are recommended for implementing Activities III, IV, and V of this unit. These are but a few of the many expressive signs of American Sign Language (ASL). The chart also includes translations of the same words in other languages. The translations may change developing on usage including formal/informal, singular/plural, and feminine/masculine. For assistance with usage and accurate pronunciation, it may be helpful to choose a language (or languages) with which you, or someone in your class or school, is familiar. Allow children to teach whenever possible.

	Spanish	Italian	Chinese (Cantonese)	Swahili	Hebrew	French	Russian
I love you	Te amo	Ti amo	Mwah Ai Ni	Nakupemba	Ani ohev (et) otcha (otach)	Je t'aime	Ia tebia liubliu
Happy	Feliz	Felice	Fieloo	Furaha	Simach	Heureux (m) Heureuse (f)	Schastlivyi (m) Schastlivaia (f)
Sad	Triste	Triste	Pei	Uzuni	Atzuv	Triste	Pechal'nyi (m) Pechal'naia (f)
Angry	Anojado (m) Anojada (f)	Arrabbiato	Naau	Kukazirika	Ka'as	Fâché (m) Fâchée (f)	Serdityi (m) Serdidataia (f)
Surprised	Sorpresa	Sorpreso	Keen Kay	Kushangaa	Hafta'ah	Etonné (m) Etonnéé (f)	Udiviennyi (m) Udiviennaia (f)
Good morning	Buenos días	Buongiorno	Choe Sun	Hujambo Hamjambo (plural)	Boker tov	Bonjour	Dobryi den'
Good night	Buenas noche	Buonanotte	Mau On	Kwaheri (good bye)	Lila tov	Bonne nuit	Dobraia noch'

I love you

Happy

Sad

Angry

Surprised

Good

morning

night

''I love you'' reproduced with permission of the American Society for Deaf Children; ''happy,'' ''sad,'' ''angry,'' ''surprised,'' ''good morning,'' and ''good night'' reproduced with permission from *Basic Sign Communication: Vocabulary* published by the National Association of the Deaf.

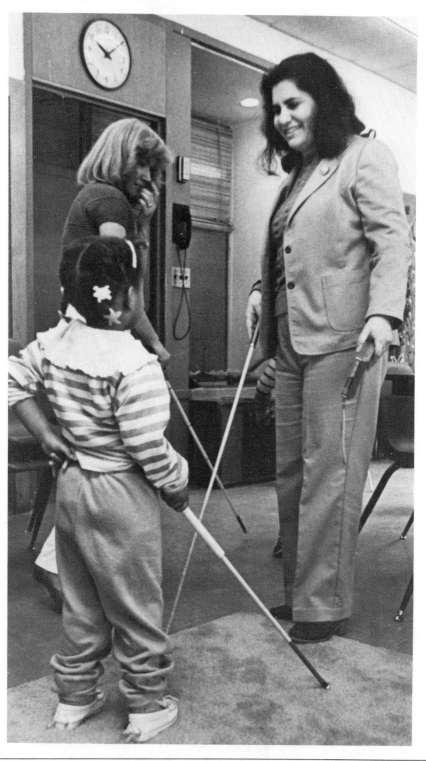

Body Parts

OVERVIEW

Understanding how all parts of the body function and feeling comfortable with one's own body are essential to a growing child's self-image. Learning about disability expands upon the traditional body parts early childhood curriculum so that in addition to learning how parts of the body function, children also learn that not all people use their bodies in the same way. This leads to good problem-solving skills and helps children learn how to use their bodies more fully.

The activities that follow extend a body parts curriculum to include the concept of visual impairment. These activities build upon the importance of hands-on sensory experiences in early childhood. By incorporating the concept of visual impairment, children learn about and use their other senses in dramatic and highly experiential ways.

As the body parts curriculum progresses, children learn about what it means to be blind. The concept of being blind is a difficult one for young children to grasp. For example, it was difficult for the children to comprehend that Ellen Rubin, a staff member of Project Inclusive who is blind and worked with the children during the pilot testing, really could not see them. They would tell her she was only fooling, and many children brought objects for her to identify. She continually assured them that she could not see and that she could tell who they were by the sound of their voices. By the end of the pilot testing, however, when Liang, a three-year-old girl from the class, was teaching Ellen how to say good-bye in American Sign Language, she realized that Ellen could not see her making the sign. Liang took Ellen's hands and helped her to place them on her body correctly.

The Body Parts curriculum activities include:

PRELIMINARY
ACTIVITY   *Learning About Our Bodies*

ACTIVITY I   *Introducing a "New Friend" and the Concept of Visual Impairment*

ACTIVITY II   *About Our Eyes*

ACTIVITY III   *Using Our Senses*

ACTIVITY IV   *A Sensory Experience*

ACTIVITY V   *Exploring the Environment with a Cane*

ACTIVITY VI   *About Braille*

Materials

Adult and child-size canes. Any local agency that provides services to people with visual impairments may have canes that are not being used.

Bodies (book). New York: E.P. Dutton, 1973.

Glasses and glasses frames without lenses. Local opticians can be your primary community resource.

My Favorite Place (book). Nashville: Abingdon Press, 1983.

"New Friend" doll (pattern). The Chapel Hill Training Outreach Project. Lincoln Center, Merritt Hill Rd., Chapel Hill, NC 27514.

Roly Goes Exploring (book). New York: Philomel Books, 1981.

Alternative Materials

Braille Alphabet. Library of Congress, Division for the Blind and Physically Handicapped, Washington, DC 20542.

Braille and Print Books. Books in a combination of Braille and print can be obtained from the following sources: *American Brotherhood for the Blind, Twin Vision Books,* 18440 Oxnard St., Tarzana, CA 91356; *Howe Press,* 175 North Beacon St., Watertown, MA 02172. In some areas of the country, the Regional Libraries of The Library of Congress, Division for the Blind and Physically Handicapped will lend books to teachers for educational purposes.

A Cane in Her Hand (book). Chicago: Albert Whitman & Co., 1977.

Touch Me Book (a Golden Touch and Feel Book). Racine, WI: Western Publishing Co., 1961.

PRELIMINARY ACTIVITY

Learning About Our Bodies

PURPOSES

- To extend children's understanding of their bodies as a whole and the parts that it contains.
- To discuss some of the functions of the human body.
- To identify what is the same and different about human bodies.

WHAT CHILDREN LEARN

- The names of parts of the body.
- The basic functions of a body.
- To discuss body functions openly.
- Similarities and differences between bodies.
- Several songs related to body parts.
- Small and large motor coordination as they perform gestures with each song.

FORMAT

A. Large- or small-group circle time for reading and discussion of book (20 minutes).
B. Large- or small-group music time for singing body parts songs (15 minutes).

MATERIALS AND SUPPLIES

Bodies

This book offers accurate information about the human body and some of its primary functions. It includes photographs of nude little boys playing in a brook, nude little girls playing in a bathtub, and a young child sitting on a toilet to illustrate that humans have to eliminate wastes. The photos are excellent and implement the premise of the book, which is to impart an understanding of the human body.

Songs

"Head and Shoulders, Knees and Toes," "Put Your Finger in the Air," "If You Are Happy and You Know It."

ACTIVITY

A. *Circle Time*

1. Introduce the book and, before reading it, have a brief discussion about the human body. Let children talk about what they know—visible body parts, internal organs, muscles.

2. Read the story. Whenever possible refer to what the children have said about the body—affirming or clarifying as needed.

3. Have a discussion after the story. Talk about different body parts; what everybody needs to do to stay healthy, e.g., eat, sleep, exercise; how bodies are alike and different.

4. Include the book *Bodies* in the classroom library.

B. *Music Time*

1. Sing a body parts song with the children. Each song should be accompanied by appropriate gestures, e.g., putting fingers or hands on appropriate body part. Afterward, relate the song to the book by reminding children of the body parts they talked about previously.

2. Continue to sing body parts songs as a part of music time.

EQUITY ISSUES

Bodies, published in 1973, is illustrated with people of diverse ages and racial/ethnic backgrounds, but it does not include people with disabilities. If, however, balanced by books that are inclusive, it is an asset to any classroom because of its frank and open view of the human body—a view not often found in children's books.

BE AWARE

Initially some children may be embarrassed by the pictures of nude children or the child shown on a toilet. Usually these are the children who have the most need for open discussion. You will need to set a tone of serious discussion that is factual and scientific. Some children may use the book as an opportunity to engage in "toilet talk." Again, the tone you set will be most important. When this book was read and discussed as part of a human body curriculum unit in a day-care center some years ago, the teacher found that after some initial embarrassment and silliness, the children engaged in far less furtive body exploration and toilet talk. Their knowledge of and interest in the human body also increased dramatically.

ALTERNATIVES

If the book *Bodies* is not available, it is still important to discuss body parts with children and to sing body parts songs.

ACTIVITY I

Introducing a "New Friend" and the Concept of Visual Impairment

PURPOSES

- To help children understand and accept that everyone's visual acuity is not the same.
- To introduce and incorporate visual aids such as glasses into the classroom environment.
- To relate visual impairment to the children's own experiences, e.g., themselves, relatives, teachers, classmates who wear glasses.

WHAT CHILDREN LEARN

- That there are varying degrees of visual acuity.
- That glasses can help many people see better.
- That people of all ages wear glasses.
- New vocabulary, e.g., disability, visual impairment.

FORMAT

A. Large-group circle time for introduction of doll (15 minutes).

B. Small groups for follow-up in dramatic play area (ongoing).

MATERIALS AND SUPPLIES

"New Friend" doll with glasses

For this curriculum area, the "New Friend" doll, made from a do-it-yourself pattern, wears a pair of child-size nonprescription glasses. It is important that these glasses have clear lenses so they appear real to the children; however, since children will be trying them on, they should not be prescription lenses. Sew a piece of elastic onto the ends of the glasses so they will fit securely around the head of the doll. This also will show how some children have their glasses held on.

Glasses frames without lenses

BACKGROUND INFORMATION

People who are visually impaired use glasses to help them see better. About one person in every four needs her or his vision corrected in some way with glasses (or contact lenses). There are many different degrees of visual impairment, however, and glasses don't always help restore vision to 20/20. For information about visual impairment, which will help to answer children's questions, see Resources section.

ACTIVITY

A. *Large-group circle time*

1. Introduce the "New Friend" doll to the children during circle time; most likely children will want to give the doll a name.

2. Ask children to talk about the doll; what do they notice about her or him? Children will probably notice the doll's glasses immediately.

3. Ask children if they know anyone who wears glasses: another child, a teacher, a family member. Most likely there will be some children in the class who wear glasses. This provides an excellent opportunity to help them feel good about themselves. Check with them beforehand, and if children agree, include them in the discussion. Have them talk about their glasses and how they obtained them.

4. Ask the children why people wear glasses. Point out that glasses help people to see more clearly. Children might talk about people who wear sunglasses. Point out that sunglasses are usually not prescription glasses; rather they are worn to help reduce the glare of the sun.

5. After discussion is completed, put the doll into the dramatic play or other appropriate area, where she or he will become a permanent part of the classroom.

B. *Dramatic Play*

1. Put glasses frames without lenses into the dramatic play area.

2. Notice the kinds of play that the glasses stimulate.

EQUITY ISSUES

For a full discussion of the equity issues involved in making a "New Friend" doll, see The Inclusive Curriculum: How To Do It. For example, it is important to dress the doll in typical play clothes suitable for both sexes, i.e., overalls and T-shirt; to give the doll a hairdo that is not obviously for a girl or a boy; to be sensitive to potential stereotyping in the ethnicity of the doll. Also, do not refer to the doll as "she" or "he" in advance, thus influencing the children's choice of name for the doll.

BE AWARE

It is important to watch out for any fears by the children in terms of playing with the glasses frames. Do not force anyone to play with glasses; instead, try to determine what is causing the fear. It simply may be that children know someone who has told them not to "play" with their glasses. Point out that these glasses are for play and that they do not have lenses. Or, it may be that the subject matter is frightening to a child. Try to reassure a child if she or he is afraid. Ask, "Why don't you want to wear glasses?" Put on the frames yourself.

Also, it is important to make sure that the children do not think the doll is wearing glasses because she or he is blind. As this curriculum develops, you will be discussing blindness with children. For now, it is sufficient to point out that people who are blind can't see; therefore they usually don't wear glasses.

ALTERNATIVES

If it is not possible to have a "New Friend" doll made, try to get glasses to fit an existing doll in the classroom.

ACTIVITY II
About Our Eyes

PURPOSES

- To extend children's understanding, through simulation, of different degrees of visual impairment.
- To have children mark on a chart and discuss their observations.

WHAT CHILDREN LEARN

- That people see things in different ways.
- To articulate information about the function of eyes.
- Vocabulary words that are specific to vision, e.g., wink, blink, blurry, sight, observe.
- How to observe and record information.

FORMAT

Pairs of children for small-group activity (10-15 minutes per pair).

MATERIALS AND SUPPLIES

2 boxes approximately 6" x 8" x 2"
e.g., cereal, cracker, or cookie box

Waxed paper

Rubber bands or tape

Pictures of bright, clearly-defined objects
e.g., any simple lotto picture

Paper and markers for chart

BACKGROUND INFORMATION

For information about visual impairment and glasses, see Activity I.

ACTIVITY

1. Prepare the viewers as follows:
   a) Empty the two boxes and place in an upright position on work surface.

b) Cut off flaps from top end of boxes.

c) Cut boxes in half across the middle, cutting parallel to the top and bottom. This will give you two sections that can be looked through when held up to eyes like viewers and two sections that cannot be looked through because the bottoms are still intact.

d) Take one of the two open-ended sections and cover one end of it with waxed paper. Fasten the waxed paper with tape or a rubber band to keep it secure. This will give a blurry image when one looks through it.

e) For the activity, you need three sections: One section that can be seen through, one section with waxed paper fastened to one end, which will give a blurry image, and one section with the bottom on that cannot be seen through.

f) Look through each of the viewers at a brightly colored picture to get an idea of what the children will see.

2. Set up one large chart on which all children will record their observations and arrange the viewers, pictures, and chart on a table (see end of activity for a sample of the chart).

3. Work with pairs of children at the table. Before experimenting with the viewers, ask the children, "What do we do with our eyes?", e.g., see, look, watch, wink, blink, cry, "How do our eyes help us?", e.g., read, play, walk.

4. Have children look at each of the viewers: first, the clear one; second, the one with waxed paper; and last, the one with the closed end. Ask them how they think the picture will look through each one. Then have them look at the picture through each of the viewers in the same order. The distance that the viewer with the waxed paper is held from the picture will determine how blurry the image is. Let children experiment with this.

5. Discuss the differences in what is seen through each of the viewers. Children may need to be assured that they are not supposed to see anything through the viewer with the closed end. Explain that people see things in different ways. People who need to wear glasses to help them see clearly might, without their glasses, see the way the picture looks through the waxed paper.

6. Have children look at the picture through the viewers again and have them record their observations on the chart, i.e., mark whether they see clearly, see blurry, or see nothing as they look through each viewer.

7. Once all children have had a chance to observe through the viewers and have marked their observations on the chart (this may occur over several days), discuss the chart in a large group. At this point, someone who wears glasses (either a child, a teacher, or a staff member) might be willing to describe what it means for them to see with and without glasses, e.g., "Without my glasses, I see the way you saw through the waxed paper. With my glasses, I see the way you saw through the open box." Be sure to use the term "visual impairment" during the discussion.

EQUITY ISSUES

This activity, in addition to its focus on visual impairment, introduces the scientific method in a simple charting activity for young children. Children first observe and then record their observations. Since, traditionally, even young boys are more encouraged in the sciences than girls, it is important that girls and boys participate equally. Try to have girl/boy pairs and be sure to use words such as observing, experimenting, and recording.

BE AWARE

For health reasons, when doing this activity, be sure that children do not let the viewers touch their eyes or their noses.

ALTERNATIVES

Instead of viewers made from boxes, frames can be made from construction paper or cardboard for children to look through. Plastic wrap or screening can be used instead of waxed paper.

CHART

	Closed end	Waxed paper	Open end
See clearly			
See blurry			
See nothing			

ACTIVITY III

Using Our Senses

PURPOSES

- To help children understand how people who are blind develop their sense of touch, hearing, taste, and smell as an alternative to their sense of sight.
- To help children develop their sense of touch.
- To help children explore the classroom and learn about things through senses other than sight.

WHAT CHILDREN LEARN

- That people who are blind learn to use senses other than sight to get around and to learn about things.
- Language skills to describe objects, e.g., hard, round, fuzzy.
- Spatial and sensory skills as they move about the classroom with their eyes closed.

FORMAT

Small groups of three to four children (10-15 minutes per group).

MATERIALS AND SUPPLIES

Viewer with closed end
(from Activity II)

Small items from the classroom
e.g., a block, a small car, a paint brush, crayon, book, puzzle piece, glasses frames

Round oatmeal box
or any other box or bag that children can fit their hands into

Blindfold (optional)

BACKGROUND INFORMATION

A person with a total loss of visual image is defined as blind. Many people think that a person who is blind has a "sixth sense" about things.

This is not true. People who are blind develop their other senses as an alternative to their sense of sight. The senses of touch, smell, taste, and hearing are used in performing daily tasks.

ACTIVITY

1. Sit down with a small group of children and have them each look through the viewer with a closed end as in Activity II. Ask them what they see. Talk about the chart that they made and how most children said that they "see nothing" when looking through this viewer. Tell children that there are people who can't see. Introduce the word "blind." Tell children that people who can't see are people who are blind.

2. Ask children if they know anyone who is blind. Children might remember seeing a person who is blind in the neighborhood. For

example, during the pilot testing, one child recalled seeing Mr. Winters, a person who uses a guide dog. Later on, Mr. Winters came to visit the class, and the children had the opportunity to ask him questions.

3. Ask children how they think people who are blind can tell where they are, or who someone is, or what is in front of them. Let children explore many possibilities. If the children don't mention it, be sure to bring the discussion around to the use of other senses, e.g., touch, smell, hearing, and taste. Then tell children that they are going to explore one of their senses—the sense of touch.

4. Place the small classroom objects (one for each child in the group) into a box or bag that has an opening for a child to put her or his hand into. Have each child reach into the box, touch an object, and guess what it is. Children should turn their heads away from the box or close their eyes when it is their turn to guess. Children may be blindfolded for this activity. One teacher put an oatmeal box into a large sock. The sock, which went up the children's arms, kept them from peeking at the objects.

5. Have the children take the objects out to see if they guessed correctly. Then have children close their eyes and feel the object and tell you what they can learn about the object from just touching it. Is it hard? Smooth? Does it have wheels? Is it square or round?

6. After all children have had a turn, talk again in a large group about how your sense of touch could help you if you could not see. For example, staff member Ellen Rubin was talking to a five-year-old class when one of the children asked her how she knew how much money she had so she didn't get cheated when she went shopping. Her explanation fascinated the children, and it is an excellent example of how the sense of touch can be used instead of the sense of sight. Ellen pointed out that coins are different enough to enable a person to readily identify them by touch. Of the four most commonly used coins, the quarter is the largest. It has a textured rim, which is made by engraved lines around the edge. Next in size is the nickel. It is smaller than the quarter but thicker and has a smooth rim. The penny is next in size, and it is also smooth. It is thinner than the nickel and just a bit smaller. Sometimes these two cause confusion when relying solely on touch. The dime is the smallest of the coins and is readily identified by the same textured rim that is on the quarter. It is also the thinnest of all the coins.

When teaching children how to tell the differences in coins by touch, it is a good idea to begin by presenting the ones that are the most different, so that it is easier to discriminate among the coins. Begin using a penny and a quarter, or a dime and a nickel, then progress from there. For older children you may want to point out the differences in weight and thickness.

Initially bills are impossible to identify on the basis of touch alone. Once someone tells a person who is blind which denomination is which, the person will generally fold or separate the bills in a consistent way. For example, leave the one-dollar bills flat, fold a five in half the short way, fold a ten into quarters (twice the fold of the five), and so forth.

EQUITY ISSUES

After age three, girls and boys often tend to segregate into same sex groups for play. This discourages girl/boy friendships, and boys begin to look upon girls as not worthy of their attention. You can help to break up these rigid same-sex groups by selecting girls and boys to work together in small groups. When girls and boys do work together, as with all groups of children, be sure that one child does not dominate the activity. Help children who may not be too verbal to express themselves, and help other children who tend to assert themselves to wait their turn. Observe your own behavior. Do you tend to call on one sex more than the other? Do you tend to call on children you know will give the "right" answers?

BE AWARE

Never force a child to be blindfolded; some children might find this frightening. When trying to guess what an object is, children may peek because they don't want to guess wrong and make a "mistake." You may have to assure them that you are not "testing" them but that they are to find out what they can learn from their sense of touch. Be sure to keep making the connection between learning by touching instead of by looking.

ALTERNATIVES

If children are willing to be blindfolded, it would be interesting to have them try to identify large objects, such as a table or chair. Guide children to the object to be identified. This will give children an experience in relation to large objects in space.

A wonderful extension of this activity is to make a touch and identify book with the class. Use familiar objects, such as a toothbrush, comb, crayon, or glasses frames, and tactile surfaces such as cotton, sandpaper, and so forth. The *Touch Me Book* is a good example of a tactile book to use with young children. Another extension is to have children identify other familiar objects through taste and smell and to listen to records of different sounds.

ACTIVITY IV

In describing his favorite place, Jon, a five-year-old child who is blind, told about a trip to the country: "I met a horse named Blaze. When I went outside, I listened for the sound of hooves as Blaze walked toward me. I knew when Blaze was close because of the smell! The best part was feeding Blaze. I put a piece of apple on my hand, and Blaze's mouth tickled and scratched me. Then Blaze's tongue grabbed the food and left my hand all sticky and wet."

A Sensory Experience

PURPOSES

- To reinforce the knowledge that adults and children who are blind use senses other than sense of sight.
- To extend children's awareness of how our senses help us learn in an outdoor environment.

WHAT CHILDREN LEARN

- How people who are blind experience and enjoy an outdoor environment through their senses other than sight.
- How to listen to, smell, touch, and taste things in the environment.
- What one can learn from senses other than sight.
- Language and recording skills as they make an experience chart about their trip.

FORMAT

A. Large-group circle time for reading the book (15 minutes).
B. Large or small group for a trip around the neighborhood (30-40 minutes).

MATERIALS AND SUPPLIES

My Favorite Place

This story is full of the multisensory experiences of a child's trip to the ocean—hearing seagulls, feeling sand, touching water. It is not until the end of the story, after many experiences familiar to all children, that the reader discovers that the girl in the story is blind.

BACKGROUND INFORMATION

Because a person who is blind learns to make greater use of the sensory clues in the environment, she or he learns to listen more carefully and to pay closer attention to things that a person who is not blind may ignore.

ACTIVITY

A. *Large-group circle time*

   1. Read *My Favorite Place* to the class. When you have finished, ask the children if they have ever been to a beach. How did the sand feel? The water sound? The sun feel? Do they have "a favorite place?" What is it like? If there is no beach nearby, pick another outdoor sensory experience to discuss.

   2. After you have read the story, talk about how the girl experienced her environment through her senses other than sight. Which senses was she using? Refer back to the children's experiences in Activity III, "Using Our Senses."

   3. After reading and discussing *My Favorite Place*, the book should be placed in the classroom library.

B. *A trip around the neighborhood*

   1. Before you go on the trip, discuss with children that, like the girl in *My Favorite Place*, they are going to use their senses of touch, smell, and hearing.

   2. Choose the route of the trip very carefully; it should allow the children to experience many familiar things in a multisensory way. For example:

   If you are in a city:

   Listen.
   Can you tell when the traffic light changes? Look at the traffic light to see if you were right. Can you tell when a bus passes? What else can you learn about your environment just by listening? Is any construction going on in the neighborhood that you visit?

Smell.

Can you identify the local bakery? Vegetable stand? Pizza place? Taco stand? Fish store? What else can you tell about your neighborhood just by smelling? Can you smell the cologne on people passing by? Can you smell the fumes from the cars and buses?

Touch.

Can you feel the sun warming you? Can you feel the wind blowing in your hair or pushing you? Can you use the sun or the wind to tell when you have come to the corner of a block with tall buildings? Can you identify a fire hydrant, a telephone pole, or a mailbox by touching them?

If you are in the country:

Listen.

Can you hear any birds? Can you hear other animals? A dog? A cow? If you can hear them, where are they? Inside or outdoors, near or far? Do your footsteps sound different on grass, a gravel path, a hard-packed dirt path? Are there leaves on the ground? Can you hear them crunching under your feet? What does that tell you about the season?

Smell.

Can you smell fresh cut grass or hay? Can you identify flowers, plants, animals?

Touch.

Can you feel the sun warming you? Can you feel the wind blowing your hair or pushing you? What does that tell you about the weather? Can you identify flowers, plants, or animals by touch?

3. After the trip around the neighborhood, make an experience chart about the trip that tells what the children heard, smelled, and touched.

EQUITY ISSUES

The discussion of children's favorite places affords the opportunity to call upon rich multicultural experiences.

The trip around the neighborhood gives children an opportunity to explore. Studies show that, beginning at birth, boys are encouraged to explore their environment more fully than girls. Children with disabilities, too, often are sheltered from exploring the outside world. Therefore, it is important to encourage all children to participate equally during the trip.

BE AWARE

Children may not understand how the girl in the story could be blind since her eyes are open. Explain that some people who are blind wear dark glasses, and some keep their eyes closed, but most people who are blind keep their eyes open.

ALTERNATIVES

If the book *My Favorite Place* is not available, the trip about the neighborhood is still an excellent activity and will stand on its own. Afterward, have children talk about other places they have been and what they are like. If appropriate, ask about a beach and have children describe their experiences there.

ACTIVITY V

> While exploring with the canes, the teacher asked Rosa, "What did you find?" Rosa answered, "A chair." Carl giggled and said, "I found something, too." Teacher: "What did you find?" Carl: "I found Rosa!"

Exploring the Environment with a Cane

PURPOSES

- To learn about one mobility aid used by people who are blind, e.g., canes.
- To explore an environment with a cane to locate and avoid obstacles.

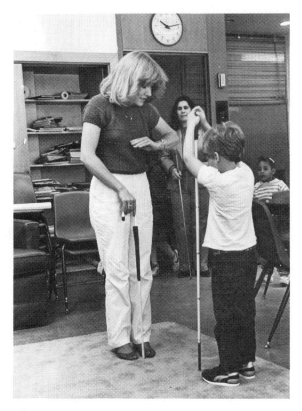

WHAT CHILDREN LEARN

- Information about how some people who are blind move about.
- To move their bodies through space in new ways.
- How senses other than sight can be used to find things that might be in the way.
- How a cane can help to locate and avoid obstacles.
- Verbal and mapping skills.

FORMAT

A. Large group discussion (10-15 minutes).

B. Small groups of two to three children (15 minutes per group).

MATERIALS AND SUPPLIES

Child-size canes
approximately 27-30 inches long

Adult-size canes
or 1/2"-3/4" dowels

BACKGROUND INFORMATION

A cane is one of the mobility aids used by people who are blind. It usually is white with a red tip. Its length is determined by the individual user's height and length of stride; usually it comes to the middle of the user's chest. For the most part, these kinds of canes are not used by very young children. For more information about mobility aids for people who are blind, see Resources section.

ACTIVITY

A. *Large-group discussion*

1. During circle time, show the canes to the children and ask them what they think they are used for. Point out that these are the kinds of canes used by some people who are blind to help them locate things near them. For example, a cane can be used to locate a table. The person may be looking for the table or want to avoid it.

2. Talk about getting around without being able to see. How does the cane help? Point out that the cane, not the person, "bumps."

3. With an adult-size cane, demonstrate how the cane is used. Hold the cane as if it were an umbrella pointed toward the ground and extend the index finger along the shaft. Move the cane in an arc in front of your body. The cane should be in front of the left foot when stepping forward with the right, and vice versa. This allows the cane to check the next step before you take it.

B. *Small-group activity*

1. Work with small groups of children over a number of days until all have had the opportunity to participate. Go over again how the cane is used, and let each child experiment holding and walking with the cane. It is not crucial that children use the cane expertly. Talk again about getting around without being able to see. How will a cane help? How will they be able to identify objects?

2. Set rules about the use of the cane. It is for walking only, no swinging in the air, no hitting, and no poking.

3. Have the children close their eyes and begin in an open area of the classroom or hallway where the cane can be clearly heard tapping on the floor. Then approach an area with a rug or other floor covering that will change the sound of the tapping. Point out the difference; sometimes on a rug the cane makes no sound. Allow children to explore.

4. Let each child walk slowly toward a classroom table and tell her or him to stop when the cane "bumps" it. This should be done with a variety of objects in the classroom (chairs, wastepaper basket, shelves). Point out the differences, compare the sounds that are made when the cane taps each different item. Be sure to include things made from metal, wood, plastic, and cardboard. You may want to clear a portion of the room for this activity or use another space with table and chairs.

5. Go into the hallway and have each child use the cane to locate a doorway or a turn in the hallway. When moving the cane in its usual arc, from left to right, be sure that one side always touches the wall. It should be easy to identify the openings because the cane is no longer stopped by the wall.

6. After all children have had the opportunity to explore with a cane, have them talk in a large group about their experiences. Draw a diagram of the area the children explored. Have collage materials available, and let children cut out tables, chairs, and so forth. Have children place the cut-outs on the diagram, thus making a tactile map of the explored areas.

EQUITY ISSUES

This activity provides an opportunity for exploration and helps children learn about spatial relationships in a new way. As in Activity III, it is important to encourage all children to participate equally, since traditionally girls and children of both sexes who are disabled are not encouraged to explore their environment. Watch for children who may be timid about exploring the space around them. Give encouragement when necessary.

BE AWARE

Children never should be blindfolded for this activity. They may become afraid and try to pull off the blindfold with the cane in their hand. Children should just close their eyes and be free to open them if they feel they need to. For some children, you may want to suggest that they try covering their eyes with a hand, so some light can be seen as they practice with the canes.

Watch out for children's confusion between a long cane that people who are blind use and canes used by people who are mobility impaired. Chances are that children will be more familiar with the latter.

ALTERNATIVES

To extend this activity, the canes can be used in the gym or other large, relatively empty room. Be sure that the children notice the different sound the cane makes tapping in the gym compared to the crowded classroom. It is also possible to experiment outdoors, noticing the different sounds the cane makes when walking on different surfaces such as grass, concrete, gravel, or protective mats in the playground.

If small canes are not available, adult-size canes can be cut down to child-size. Shave the end so the tip will fit back on and wrap it with reflecting tape. If canes are not available, it is possible to use ½"-¾" dowels. Be sure to add reflecting tape to simulate a cane's tip.

For older children, the book *A Cane in Her Hand* would be a good follow-up to the small group activity. During the discussion, you could talk about the cane as a "tool." The book describes a long cane like "a long arm . . . that helps find low things before you bump into them."

The following matching game could be used as a follow-up to the children's experimenting with canes. Place two small pieces of wood, tile, plastic, and so forth on a table. With a small stick, have each child (without looking) tap on each surface, listen, and then tap on the next. Have children match pieces by the sounds they make.

ACTIVITY VI

Teacher: "Who reads Braille?" One of the children answers: "Fingers!"

About Braille

PURPOSES

- To expand awareness of learning through touch.
- To introduce Braille, one system that enables some people who are blind to read.

WHAT CHILDREN LEARN

- Information about reading and writing in Braille.
- That one can get information through touch.
- That some people "read" through touch and listening, e.g., Braille and tapes.
- Numbers and shapes recognition.

FORMAT

Large group circle time (15 minutes).

MATERIALS AND SUPPLIES

Roly Goes Exploring

This simple but delightful story about Roly, a circle that goes exploring, is an exceptional early childhood resource. The text is in Braille as well as in print and can be enjoyed by all children, blind and sighted. The "pictures" on each page are cut-outs that can be felt as well as seen, providing a wonderful tactile experience.

BACKGROUND INFORMATION

Braille is a series of raised dots that form letters. It is a system that enables persons who are blind to read by running their fingers over a line of Braille. See Resources section for further information.

ACTIVITY

1. Read *Roly Goes Exploring* to the class.

2. Ask children what they notice about this book. Most likely, children will notice the Braille and cut-out pictures almost immediately. If children haven't noticed it, point out the Braille. Tell children that Braille is a series of raised dots and that the letters of the alphabet are represented in Braille. Books are printed in Braille so that people who are blind can read them by touch.

3. Be sure that children have the opportunity to touch the Braille and the cut-outs in the book. Children should place their hands and fingers on the Braille, as a fingernail might rub it out.

4. After reading and discussing *Roly*, the book should be placed in the class library.

EQUITY ISSUES

Although *Roly Goes Exploring* is a good resource, it has two flaws. One, *Roly* is referred to as "he" throughout. This is a telling example of the discriminative use of "he" as a generic pronoun, since there is nothing in the story that would make *Roly*—a circle—either male or female. Young children understand the world around them in literal ways. Studies have shown that children do not understand that the pronoun "he" refers universally to all people. Likewise, when police officers are referred to as policemen, children infer that only men can be police officers. To mitigate this, you can change the "he" to "it" in

Roly, or you can alternate readings of the book referring to Roly as "she." Discussing with the children why you are doing this is an excellent way to begin to help children understand the meaning of stereotypes. *Roly's* second flaw is that on the last page of the book, the Braille alphabet appears as printed, not raised dots. This is a shame, since the rest of the book is accessible to children who are blind.

BE AWARE

Children may refer to the Braille as "bumps" or "dots." This is acceptable, as long as you remind them each time that the "bumps" or "dots" are called Braille.

ALTERNATIVES

Roly Goes Exploring is worth having in any classroom. However, it is possible to obtain other books in a combination of Braille and print from American Brotherhood for the Blind, Twin Vision Books, the Howe Press, and some regional branches of the Library of Congress, Division for the Blind and Physically Handicapped.

Another way to introduce Braille, especially for older children, is by making a tactile Braille alphabet chart with lens-shaped styrofoam packaging materials glued onto colorful oaktag. This kind of styrofoam also can be used as one of the classroom art materials that children can use in collages and when they write their names. It is an excellent way to make the classroom inclusive with inexpensive, readily available materials. If styrofoam is not available, buttons, paper fasteners, or any other uniform, round, raised objects may be used.

To make the Braille chart, you will need a large sheet of oaktag approximately 22" × 28", lens-shaped styrofoam packaging materials, Elmer's Glue, magic marker, and a copy of the chart (see end of activity). Divide the oaktag into four horizontal rows of approximately 5½" each. Each row will contain printed letters with Braille letters placed underneath. You can easily fit six or seven letters on a line if the oaktag is 28" wide. Print the letters of the alphabet with a pencil, making the letters 1½"-2" high for easy reading. Allow two to four inches between letters, depending on how many dots a Braille letter contains. Mark the print equivalent under each letter. Adjust spacing so that each letter is clearly differentiated from the letter next to it. (Some Braille letters are wider than others.) When you are satisfied with the spacing, go over the pencilled print letters with a marker. Place a circle of glue in the space for each Braille dot and also run a little glue around the edge of the styrofoam with your finger. Glue each Braille letter down. After the chart dries thoroughly, mount it on a wall at the children's eye level. Copies of the Braille alphabet are available from the Library of Congress, Division for the Blind and Physically Handicapped.

AN INCLUSIVE ALPHABET CHART

A Braille alphabet chart can be made with simple "found" materials and colorful oaktag. Children can be encouraged to use the chart and materials to create letters and their names in Braille (see Activity VI).

a	b	c	d	e
f	g	h	i	j
k	l	m	n	o
p	q	r	s	t
u	v	w	x	y
		z		

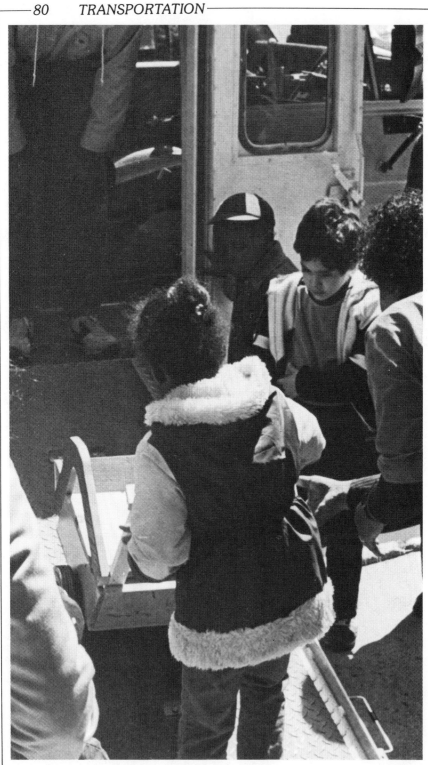

TRANSPORTATION

OVERVIEW

- How do braces and crutches help people walk?
- Why is a wheelchair like a bicycle or a car?
- How do ramps help things with wheels go from one level to another?
- What is the meaning of accessibility?

The activities that follow extend a transportation curriculum to include the concept of mobility impairment. Through direct experience with braces, crutches, and wheelchairs, children begin to understand that there are many different ways to move from one place to another. The activities increase cognitive growth in block building, foster spatial awareness, and introduce the concept of technology and how it helps people.

The activities also help children to look at their environment in new ways. As children take trips around the neighborhood looking for curb cuts and ramps, and as they measure doorways in their school to see if a person in a wheelchair can get through, they become aware of the importance of an accessible environment for all people. In one class, after the children took a trip around the school, the teacher asked, "Can you get in and out of the building if you used a wheelchair to get around?" "Yes," the children replied. "Were the doors wide enough?" "Yes," they replied again. Then one five-year-old added, "But if it's raining or cold, it would be hard because you have to go all around the building to the entrance with no stairs."

The Transportation curriculum activities include:

PRELIMINARY
ACTIVITY   *Making Footprints*

ACTIVITY I   *Introducing a "New Friend" and the Concept of Mobility Impairment*

ACTIVITY II   *Walking with Braces and Crutches*

ACTIVITY III   *Things with Wheels*

ACTIVITY IV   *Building an Accessible Block City with Ramps*

ACTIVITY V   *An Accessibility Trip Around the School*

ACTIVITY VI   *Positive Images*

Materials

Child-size crutches and a wheelchair. Physical therapy departments of local hospitals or organizations that have equipment pools for people with disabilities may be able to provide these items. It may also be possible to borrow or rent them.

Danny's Song (book). Northbrook, IL: Hubbard, 1975.

Darlene (book). New York: Methuen, 1980.

If You Thought the Wheel Was a Good Idea — You'll Love The Ramp (Feeling Free poster series). Human Policy Press, P.O. Box 127, Syracuse, NY 13210.

"New Friend" doll (pattern). The Chapel Hill Training Outreach Project, Lincoln Center, Merritt Hill Rd., Chapel Hill, NC 27514.

Sports and Spokes Magazine (pictures). 5201 North 19 Ave., Suite 111, Phoenix, AZ 85015.

Alternative Materials

Any Questions? and *We All Fit In* (Feeling Free poster series). Human Policy Press, P.O. Box 127, Syracuse, NY 13210.

Child-size walkers and helmets (see crutches and wheelchairs above).

The 52 Association (pictures). 441 Lexington Ave., New York, NY 10017.

Hospital Play Equipment (wheelchair). Victor C. Dye, Hospital Play Equipment Co., 1122 Judson Ave., Evanston, IL 60202.

Resource Photos for Mainstreaming: Children & Adult Sets. Women's Action Alliance, 370 Lexington Ave., New York, NY 10017.

Special Friends (stuffed animal in wheelchair). Pediatric Projects, Inc., P.O. Box 1880, Santa Monica, CA 90406. (213) 393-4260. Also from: The Able Child, 325 West 11 St., New York, NY 10014.

PRELIMINARY ACTIVITY

Making Footprints

PURPOSES
- To raise awareness of individual differences.
- To introduce creeping and walking as a means of transportation.

WHAT CHILDREN LEARN
- Awareness of their bodies and how they move through space.
- Different ways to move from one place to another.
- About parts of the body and their relationships to each other, particularly hands, legs, feet, and toes.
- Observation skills as they sort footprints into categories.
- Math skills, e.g., estimation and measurement.

FORMAT
A. Large-group circle time (10 minutes).
B. Small groups for printmaking and cutting (30-40 minutes).

MATERIALS AND SUPPLIES
Large pieces of brown paper
Magic markers and/or washable paint
Construction paper

ACTIVITY
A. *Large-group circle time*
  1. Ask children how, when they were babies, they were able to get from one place to another, e.g., creeping. Have children take turns creeping from one side of the circle to the other.

2. Lay a large piece of brown paper in the center of the circle and ask children what parts of their bodies would be represented on the paper if they made a print of a child in a creeping position.

3. Ask one child to be the model and creep onto the brown paper. Trace the parts of her or his body that are touching the paper, i.e., hands and legs from knee to foot. Have children examine the print. Had they guessed correctly?

4. Ask children how they think the print would look if they were walking.

5. Trace several children's footsteps when walking on the brown paper and compare their length of stride.

6. Guess what the prints would look like for hopping and jumping. Trace several children's footsteps when hopping and jumping on the brown paper. Some children may need support as they will have to hop (and trace), hop (and trace), jump (and trace), jump (and trace), and so on.

7. Compare tracings. When are the feet far apart? When are the feet close together? When is there only one print? What is the difference in stride when walking, hopping, and jumping? How can you recognize the difference between walking and hopping in the tracing?

B. **Small group printmaking**

1. Work with groups of two or three children. Ask the children to take off their shoes and socks. Have each child make a print with washable paint of one foot on a piece of brown paper. (If it is not possible to use paints, trace children's feet instead.)

2. Note overall size—length and width—of each foot. Note length of toes. Some feet have longer big toes, while others have longer second toes.

3. When all the children have made footprints (this may take several days), cut out the prints and line them up side by side. Have children pick out the feet with longer big toes, longer second toes, those that are wider, shorter, and so forth. Children can then sort the prints into the various categories.

4. Introduce concept of measuring and estimating by using cut-out feet, heel-to-toes to measure the room. Allow children to estimate how many "feet" it will take to cross the room in all directions.

5. Make the prints into a book by gluing cut-outs onto construction paper and labeling each with a child's name.

EQUITY ISSUES

Be sure that all children participate equally. Ask girls and boys to demonstrate crawling, walking, hopping, and jumping. Be sure that girls and boys all have a chance to estimate and measure. Teachers report that many girls still come to their centers dressed in clothing inappropriate for play and are warned "not to get dirty." It is important that all children have the opportunity to experience making feet paintings. You may have to assure some children that the paint will wash off, you may want to talk to parents in advance about the importance of sending girls to school in washable play clothes, or you may want to have sets of extra play clothes in your center for use on just such occasions.

BE AWARE

If differences in footprints are not very large, it may be difficult for children to notice subtle variations. In this case, it would be a good idea to include teachers' prints as well.

ALTERNATIVES

Working in small groups, make prints or tracings of the children's shoes. Are the number of "feet" needed to cross the room the same? Make tire prints using a variety of wheeled things in the classroom (wagon, toy car or truck). If possible, take a walk outdoors and look for prints of feet, tires, or animals. How were they made? By leaving an imprint in the ground or snow? Or by walking or riding through some mud?

ACTIVITY I

Introducing a "New Friend" and the Concept of Mobility Impairment

PURPOSES

- To introduce the concept of mobility impairment.
- To help children understand that everyone does not move about in the same way.
- To introduce children to one type of mobility aid, i.e., braces.
- To create a class story incorporating the concept of mobility impairment.

WHAT CHILDREN LEARN

- Information about mobility impairment.
- Information about braces as a mobility aid.
- Creative and verbal skills as they make up a story.

FORMAT

Large-group circle time for introduction of doll (15-20 minutes).

MATERIALS AND SUPPLIES

"New Friend" doll with leg brace(s)

The pattern for this doll comes with suggestions for making a representation of leg braces. You can also make your own adaptations. For example, Project Inclusive made a leg brace to fit the doll from a piece of metal track ordinarily used for hanging files in a drawer. The track was bent to fit around the bottom of the doll's foot. Two strips cut from leather belts and two buckles held the "brace" in place around the doll's leg.

BACKGROUND INFORMATION

There are many different kinds of mobility impairment. Braces are one device used by some people with orthopedic impairments. Braces usually are hinged to allow mobility at leg joints. For information about mobility impairment, which will help to answer children's questions, see Resources section.

ACTIVITY

1. Introduce the "New Friend" doll to the children during circle time; most likely children will want to give the doll a name.

2. Ask children to talk about the doll; what do they notice about her or him? Children might notice the brace, but not understand what it is for. Do children know anyone who wears a brace? If a child in your class wears a brace, check beforehand to see if she or he would be willing to talk about it. How does the brace work? Why does she or he wear it? Be sure that, by the end of the discussion, children understand that some people who have a mobility impairment wear braces to help them walk.

3. Have children make up a story about the doll going to school. Begin the story with:

    It is the first day of school, and (doll's name) just woke up and got out of bed. "Time to get dressed," father calls. What does (doll's name) do next?

    If the children get stuck, ask leading questions such as, "Where is (doll's name) going next?" "How is (doll's name) getting to school?" "What will (doll's name) do first at school?"

4. Make an experience chart of the children's story. Some children may want to draw pictures on the chart.

5. After the story is completed, put the doll in the dramatic play or other appropriate area, and hang the story at child's eye level in the same area.

EQUITY ISSUES

For a full discussion of the equity issues involved in making a "New Friend" doll, see The Inclusive Curriculum: How To Do It. For example, it is important to dress the doll in typical play clothes suitable for both sexes, i.e., overalls and T-shirt; to give the doll a hairdo that is not obviously for a girl or for a boy; to be sensitive to potential stereotyping in the ethnicity of the doll. Also, do not refer to the doll as "she" or "he" in advance, thus influencing the children's choice of name for the doll.

As children make up the story, watch out for any sex-role stereotyping. For example, children might say that the doll "can't play with trucks because she is a girl" or "can't cry because he is a boy." Don't let such statements pass. Ask children why they think that to be true. Don't they know a girl or boy who does these things? If they say they don't, point out that you do and move the story in this direction.

The same would be true if, in the course of the story, any racist statements are made by the children. Do not let these pass, and watch for subtle ways that children may express discomfort with race/ethnicity. These might be a comment on the color of the doll's "skin" or, as happened in the pilot testing, a child stating that he "did not like the doll's hair." The teacher pointed out that the doll, whose hair was corn-rowed, had hair very much like the hair of other children in the class. She then used this opportunity to talk about all the children's hair, how they were all different from each other, but all beautiful nonetheless.

Also, watch out that in the story the children don't make the doll appear helpless because of her or his disability. The emphasis should be on all the things the doll can do, rather than the things she or he cannot do. Be sure to focus on the role of mobility aids and the overall accessibility of the environment.

BE AWARE

Children may have a tendency to treat the doll as a baby during dramatic play, or they may make the doll passive while they are active. Suggest ways that the doll can actively take part in the dramatic play. Children may have to be encouraged to remove and put back on the brace, especially when putting the doll to sleep.

ALTERNATIVES

If it is not possible to have a "New Friend" doll made, you can make a brace to fit one of the existing dolls in the classroom.

In a classroom where children had no prior experience with disability, the children were extremely careful of their "New Friend" doll who they had named Judy. They even planned trips to the doctor to put her shoe back on so they wouldn't hurt her. As the curriculum developed, the children's attitudes toward Judy became more positive. Pretty soon, children were taking off Judy's brace when it was time to sleep, and they were taking her on trips to the park as well.

ACTIVITY II

Walking with Braces and Crutches

PURPOSES

- To promote an understanding of the feelings and activities that all children share.
- To reinforce knowledge about braces.
- To introduce crutches as another kind of mobility aid.
- To help children understand that people who are mobility impaired can do many things.

WHAT CHILDREN LEARN

- That someone who is mobility impaired and someone who is not share many similar activities and feelings.
- That a person who uses a brace and/or crutches can do many things.
- That everyone feels angry, hurt, and left out sometimes, whatever the reason.

FORMAT

A. Large-group circle time for reading of book (15 minutes).

B. Small groups for follow-up with crutches (10-15 minutes per group).

MATERIALS AND SUPPLIES

Danny's Song
This book about a boy who wears braces and uses crutches stresses the many things he does well, and they are things that children will identify with: making cocoa, playing the piano, blowing balloons, using the telephone, and so forth. The story also deals with the frustrations that Danny experiences, not because he cannot do things, but because he has to do some things more slowly.

Child-size crutches

BACKGROUND INFORMATION

Braces and crutches are two of the mobility aids used by some people with orthopedic disabilities for balance and support. The two basic types of crutches are the underarm, or auxiliary, crutch, and the forearm, or Canadian or Lofstrand, crutch.

ACTIVITY

A. *Large-group circle time*

1. Read *Danny's Song* to the class during circle time.

2. Ask children some of the following questions: What are some of the things that Danny can do? Do you do some of these things? What else can you do? How did Danny show his feelings? Why did he use braces and crutches? What did they help him do?

3. If children do not make the connection between Danny and their doll with a brace, ask them, "Do you know anyone else who wears a brace?" There might also be children in the center, family members, or teachers who use braces.

4. Bring the doll to the circle along with the child-size crutches. Show the children the crutches. Do they know anyone who uses crutches? Explain that, just as their doll has a brace, some people who are mobility impaired use braces and/or crutches for support and balance when walking. Danny used both braces and crutches. If any children in the class use crutches, check beforehand to see if they would like to talk about their crutches and to demonstrate how they are used.

5. Tell children that in small groups, over the next few days, everyone will have a turn to use the classroom crutches.

6. When discussion is completed, place *Danny's Song* in the classroom library.

B. *Small-group activity with crutches*

1. Before children use crutches, talk again about why people need to use them. Review that crutches are one means of transportation for people who are mobility impaired.

2. Work with small groups of children over a period of time until everyone has had a chance to use the crutches. Ask children what muscles they are using when they walk with crutches.

EQUITY ISSUES

Danny's Song is an excellent inclusive resource because it focuses on the many things Danny can do well, while acknowledging that he can be frustrated by having to do some things more slowly. All children have strengths and weaknesses, and, therefore, they will empathize with Danny's situation. The classroom discussion should focus on what children in the class like to do and can do. Danny also is portrayed as sensitive and able to express his feelings. Be sure to point out during the discussion that all children feel sad and lonely at times, to help counteract the stereotype that boys have to hold back their emotions and "act like a man." Also, be careful that boys do not dominate in using the crutches; make sure girls have an equal chance.

BE AWARE

Supervise children very carefully as they use the crutches. The crutches will need to be adjusted and scaled down so that they are as close to the children's size as possible. Let children use both legs if need be to avoid falling. Set safety rules, such as no swinging the crutches in the air, no hitting, no poking. Point out that crutches are mobility aids, not toys. Use your judgment about leaving the crutches as part of the classroom dramatic play equipment. If children are having difficulty using them, it would be best to have children use them under supervision only. Children may be more familiar with the use of crutches for a temporary injury. You may need to point out the permanent nature of the use of crutches for support and balance by people who are mobility impaired.

ALTERNATIVES

A child-size walker used by children with orthopedic disabilities can be brought into the classroom. Since a walker is easier for children to use, it could be placed in the dramatic play area. A child-size helmet used by some children with orthopedic disabilities would be another excellent addition to the dramatic play area.

There are several good pictures and posters available that depict children and adults wearing braces and using crutches. It is strongly recommended that you hang these at children's eye level to stimulate further discussion and to help make the classroom environment more inclusive. These resources include photographs in both the children and adult sets of _Resource Photos for Mainstreaming_ and the posters _Any Questions?_ and _We All Fit In_ from the Feeling Free poster series. See Resources section for additional sources of active photographs of people who are mobility impaired.

> After having read _Danny's Song_, one child leaned over to a friend and said, "I can make cocoa, too, and I can color. But I can't play the piano."

ACTIVITY III

Things with Wheels

PURPOSES

- To demonstrate how wheels help move things from one place to another.

- To extend the traditional curriculum about wheeled objects to include wheelchairs.

- To help children understand the different purposes of wheels: to carry heavy objects, to go faster, to go long distances, to allow people to ride when they don't want to walk or can't walk.

WHAT CHILDREN LEARN

- What wheels do.
- Why wheels are important.
- The purpose of a wheelchair and other wheeled objects.
- Observation skills as they search for wheeled objects around the room.
- Categorization and math skills as they make sets.

FORMAT

Large-group circle time and collage making (20-30 minutes).

MATERIALS AND SUPPLIES

Pictures of Wheeled Objects

Collect as large a variety of pictures as possible, but be sure to include several types of wheelchairs. Photographs of athletes (adults and children) using wheelchairs are available for purchase and on loan from *Sports and Spokes* magazine. Other pictures might include bicycles, trucks, buses, cars, trains, roller skates, wagons, shopping carts, baby carriages, adult tricycles, unicycles, and scooter boards.

BACKGROUND INFORMATION

Wheelchairs come in many sizes and shapes and are adapted to the lifestyle of the user. Wheelchairs range from basic utility models for use in hospitals and airports to custom-designed models for sports activities. There are also motorized or electric wheelchairs that are battery operated.

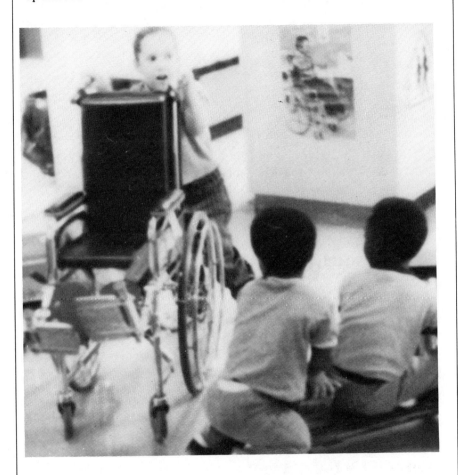

ACTIVITY

1. Collect a variety of pictures of wheeled objects that include several kinds of wheelchairs.

2. Lay out pictures on a table and, one at a time, have children come up and select the picture they want.

3. Have children bring their pictures to the circle. Go around the circle and have children describe the objects in the pictures they have

selected. Ask, "What is it called?" "What is it used for?" "What does it carry?" If no child has selected a picture of a wheelchair, you should bring it to the circle. Explain that some people use a wheelchair to get from one place to another. Ask children if they know anyone who uses a wheelchair.

4. Talk about the importance of wheels. Wheeled vehicles help get people from one place to another when they can't walk, when they need to carry heavy things, when they don't want to walk, or when they want to go long distances. To demonstrate, pull a wagon to show how much easier it is to move a heavy item from one place to another.

5. As an extension of the discussion, have children form groups according to different sets of the wheeled objects, e.g., all objects with four wheels, with two wheels, that carry a lot of people, that carry one person, that carry things, that go faster, that go slower.

6. Once the discussion is completed, work with half the class at a time and have children make a Things with Wheels collage with their pictures. Children can add to the collage with other pictures.

7. When the collage is finished, have children match objects from the classroom with the collage pictures.

EQUITY ISSUES

Traditionally, cars and trucks are thought of as typical "boys' toys." Try to avoid letting children select a sexist division of objects, e.g., boys selecting cars and trucks and girls selecting carriages and shopping carts.

BE AWARE

All the pictures should be realistic, not abstract, representations of objects. Be sure that several pictures of wheelchairs are used in making the collage.

ALTERNATIVES

Other sources for pictures of people in wheelchairs are the 52 Association and *Resource Photos for Mainstreaming: Adult Set*.

A good extension of the discussion and making the collage would be to have children use wheeled objects outdoors: ride tricycles, push carriages, pull wagons. If a child in your classroom uses a wheelchair, and if she or he has agreed beforehand, this would be an excellent opportunity for her or him to demonstrate how it is used. If at all possible, have a wheelchair available for the children to use during this activity (see Activity V).

ACTIVITY IV

*Building an Accessible
Block City with Ramps*

PURPOSES

- To introduce the concept of accessibility.
- To structure block play so that children can explore the many purposes of ramps, including accessibility.
- To reinforce knowledge of the function of wheeled objects.

WHAT CHILDREN LEARN

- The term accessible and its meaning.
- The purposes of ramps.
- The relationship of ramps to wheeled vehicles.
- The importance of accessibility for people with mobility impairments.
- Problem-solving skills as they build accessible block structures and experiment with angles of ramps.

FORMAT

A. Large-group circle time (15 minutes).

B. Small-group work in block area (ongoing).

MATERIALS AND SUPPLIES

If You Thought the Wheel Was a Good Idea — You'll Love the Ramp

This poster, one of the Feeling Free poster series, shows children using a variety of wheeled vehicles, including a tricycle, a baby carriage, a skate board, and a wheelchair.

Blocks for making ramps

Small teacher-made wheelchair and other wheeled objects such as cars and trucks

To make a wheelchair, you will need a sturdy small wooden chair with four legs and rungs, e.g., dollhouse or miniature hobbyist furniture; four wheels, preferably two small and two larger ones; and thin metal dowels to make the axles. All these materials are available in shops that cater to miniature house hobbyists.

Cut the dowels to a length long enough to fit the width of the chair, allowing a little space on either side of the chair legs so the wheels can be attached and move freely. Fit the axles through the wheels and fasten them to the front and back rungs of the chair with twist ties or other flexible wire. (Be sure ends of wire are not sharp.) Bend the dowel back with pliers to secure each wheel in place.

Miniatures of wheeled objects

e.g., doll-house sized stroller, wagon, etc.

BACKGROUND INFORMATION

Both attitudinal and architectural barriers keep people with disabilities from full participation in society. Federal laws such as Section 504 of the Rehabilitation Act of 1973 and state and local building codes mandate specifications for making buildings and facilities accessible to and usable by people with disabilities.

For a building to be accessible to a person using a wheelchair, exterior and interior space must be considered. A person must be able to get into the building, get around the building once inside, and use the bathrooms, water fountains, telephones, and elevator buttons.

ACTIVITY

A. **Large-group circle time**

1. Put up the poster *If You Thought the Wheel Was a Good Idea — You'll Love the Ramp* at children's eye level near the circle.

2. Remind children of their discussion of Things with Wheels (Activity III): how useful wheels are, how helpful they are to carry something from one place to another, and so forth. Then, ask children: What happens if you are pushing a shopping cart, or a baby carriage, or pulling a wagon, or are in a wheelchair and you have to go up some steps? Let children problem-solve through discussion.

3. After children have explored all possibilities, point out the poster featuring ramps. Ask one of the children to describe the poster. Ask if anyone has ever seen or used a ramp. Point out that ramps help things on wheels move easily from one level to another.

4. Introduce the word "accessible." Explain that a ramp helps make a building accessible to people using wheelchairs.

B. ***Small-group work in block area***

1. Tell children that for a few days, when they build in the block area, they are going to build an accessible city, i.e., one in which people in wheelchairs could move about freely.

2. Move the *If You Thought the Wheel Was a Good Idea —
   You'll Love the Ramp* poster to the block area.

3. Be sure that there are several small wheeled objects in the
   blockbuilding area as props, e.g., teacher-made wheelchair,
   cars, trucks, miniature stroller and wagon.

4. As children build, ask them appropriate questions such as:
   How will a person in a wheelchair get into the building? How
   will cars get into the garage? Allow children to experiment with
   angles of ramps.

EQUITY ISSUES

Block play is an important early childhood experience that builds early
visual spatial skills. Understanding how ramps work, for example, is
one of the basic concepts in physics. Since, traditionally, boys gravitate
to the block area more frequently than girls, it is important to make
sure that the small-group work in the block area includes a mix of girls
and boys. All children should have an equal chance to build the city in
the block area. This may have to take place over several days.

BE AWARE

Children may need to be encouraged to actually wheel the wheelchair
up a ramp into their building or the car up a ramp into their garage.
Their tendency may be to just pick up the wheelchair or car and place it
in the building or garage, even if a ramp has been built for that purpose.

ALTERNATIVES

If the *If You Thought the Wheel Was a Good Idea — You'll Love the
Ramp* poster is not available for the circle time discussion, either find
other pictures of ramps or build a ramp with blocks to demonstrate
how ramps help wheeled objects move from one level to another.

If you have money available to purchase materials, there are two
resources for obtaining wooden wheelchairs. Their drawbacks are that
they are fairly expensive and that they are on a scale larger than unit
blocks. One wheelchair (with a monkey) is available from *Special
Friends*, a series of animals with disabilities along with their disability
aids. Another wheelchair can be obtained from *Hospital Play Equipment*. For this curriculum, however, to avoid the notion that people
with disabilities are "sick," do not use other hospital-related items. The
other items could be used at another time during the year.

ACTIVITY V

An Accessibility Trip Around the School

PURPOSES

- To reinforce children's understanding of accessibility.
- To take a trip to determine if the school/center building is accessible.
- To begin to build a sense of advocacy in children.

WHAT CHILDREN LEARN

- First-hand experience about accessibility.
- Observation and recording skills as they take their accessibility trip.
- Language art skills as they compose a letter.
- Social consciousness as they advocate for accessibility.

FORMAT

Large- or small-group trips around the school (30 minutes).

MATERIALS AND SUPPLIES

Wheelchair
If possible, try to obtain a wheelchair on loan from a hospital, rehabilitation center, ambulance company, or airport.

Other Wheeled Objects
e.g., baby carriage, shopping cart, wagon.

Paper and markers for chart

BACKGROUND INFORMATION

For a school to be accessible, the following need to be considered: abrupt changes in level such as steps and curbs; uneven surfaces; narrow, heavy doors; height of water fountains, sinks, telephones, and elevator buttons; and any space that is too small to maneuver a wheelchair (corridors, bathrooms, doorways). For general information about accessibility, see Activity IV and Information About Mobility Impairment in the Resources section.

ACTIVITY

1. Before you go on the trip, talk again about the meaning of accessible. Talk about the accessible city the children built (Activity IV). Tell the children that they are going to go on a trip around the school to see if it is accessible, i.e., if someone in a wheelchair could go everywhere in the building.

2. Prepare a chart so that children can document what is and is not accessible during their trip (see end of activity for a sample of the chart).

3. Take along a few wheeled items so children can experience first hand what it means for a building to be accessible; have some children push a baby carriage, others a shopping cart. If at all possible, include a wheelchair. This way, children will be able to experience if a person using a wheelchair could pass through doorways, turn around in the corridors, use the bathrooms, or get a drink of water. If a wheelchair is not available, it would be best to focus on accessibility in terms of steps. During the trip ask: Could a person in a wheelchair get into the building? How could a person in a wheelchair get to the gym on the second floor? and so forth.

4. After all the class has gone on the trip, hang up the chart, and talk about the trip in a large group. Talk about what would have to be done to make the whole building accessible.

5. Have children write a letter to the director of the center about their trip. It could begin, "Dear Ms. _____, We took a trip around the school to see if our building is accessible to someone using a wheelchair. We wanted you to know where someone in a wheelchair could go and where someone in a wheelchair couldn't go at our school. For example: _____."

6. If, as a result of the children's trip and letter, some area of the center is made accessible, be sure to include the children—have them watch, talk to the people involved, tell them about their letter. If possible, take before and after photographs and have children make a book out of their experiences.

EQUITY ISSUES

All children should participate equally in the trip, the documentation, and the follow-up discussion. If children's actions do help to turn an inaccessible area into an accessible one, it will help them begin to understand the meaning and importance of advocacy and action.

BE AWARE

Children should understand that, while they were able to build ramps in their block city, it is not so easy to build a ramp into a real building. There are very strict regulations for constructing ramps so that they will be safe for a person using a wheelchair. For example, there have to be large level platforms at the top, bottom, and wherever a person might change direction. Too steep a ramp can be dangerous or difficult for a person using a wheelchair.

ALTERNATIVES

Once children have taken an accessibility trip around their school, they could branch out and take a trip to see if the neighborhood is accessible. Are there special parking spaces, are there corner cuts at curb crossings, are there ramps into buildings, what height are counter tops in stores? Look for signs (usually a wheelchair on a blue background) indicating that something is accessible.

*Use pictures of items where possible	accessible	not accessible
stairs	_____	_____
phone booth	_____	_____
doors	_____	_____
water fountains	_____	_____
elevator	_____	_____

ACTIVITY VI

After reading the book *Darlene*, the teacher asked, "Can you think of another game Darlene and her cousin could have played?" Lenny responded, "They could play baseball. Darlene could catch." Maryann quickly added, "She could bat, too!"

Positive Images

PURPOSES

- To provide children with a positive image of a child with a mobility impairment.
- To strengthen children's listening and discussion skills.
- To provide an opportunity for children to talk about feelings.

WHAT CHILDREN LEARN

- That a child in a wheelchair can do many active things.
- That all children experience similar feelings.
- How to talk about feelings.
- Listening and discussion skills.
- Small motor skills as they draw pictures related to the story.

FORMAT

Large-group circle time (20 minutes).

MATERIALS AND SUPPLIES

Darlene

This story is about a young girl named Darlene, who uses a wheelchair and is feeling homesick while spending a morning with her uncle and cousin. Darlene resists her cousin's attempts to play with her, but finally becomes absorbed in games and in her uncle's guitar playing. In typical fashion, when Darlene's mother arrives, Darlene doesn't want to go home.

Crayons and paper

BACKGROUND INFORMATION

For general information on mobility impairment, see Resources section.

ACTIVITY

1. Read *Darlene* to children during circle time. Do not show pictures at first, and tell children that they are to practice listening. Pictures will be shown when the story is reread.

2. After reading the story, ask children questions about it. Some sample questions: How did Darlene feel? Why? Have you ever felt the way Darlene felt? What are some of the things she did? If you were Darlene, what are some of the things you would do?

3. After discussion, show children cover of book. If children express surprise at seeing Darlene in a wheelchair, discuss this with them. Why are they surprised? Did they think Darlene would not be able to do the things she did? Or feel the way she felt?

4. After children's questions are all answered, reread the story showing them the pictures. Ask children to describe some of the pictures.

5. One of the choices during work time could be to have children draw pictures of one thing that Darlene did while at her uncle's house.

EQUITY ISSUES

The book *Darlene* is an excellent inclusive resource because: a) It does not make Darlene's disability the main focus of the story; b) It depicts a Black family; c) It includes a male caregiver as a main character; and d) It addresses a situation that is common to many children and deals with children's feelings in such a situation.

BE AWARE

During the discussion, be sure to focus on the things that Darlene can do. Children need to understand that although Darlene may do things differently, it doesn't mean she can't do them well.

ALTERNATIVES

When reading *Darlene* to younger children, you might want to read the story and show them the pictures at the same time. You could ask the same questions: How did Darlene feel? Why? Have you ever felt the way Darlene felt? and so forth.

Meeting Your Needs

While the preceding activities have all been successfully pilot tested, you may find that they need to be adapted or modified to best meet your, and your class's, individual needs. The following steps can help you do this and, at the same time, give you some idea of the effects the activities are having in your classroom.

ASSESS YOUR NEEDS

Tools that can help you assess your needs are the General Classroom Information sheet and the Checklist for an Inclusive Environment that follow. First, complete the General Classroom Information sheet. Then answer the following questions:

1. Do any of the topic areas and class trips you have scheduled deal specifically with disabilities? Do any of the curriculum activities in this guide fit into the topic areas you are planning to cover?

2. Do any children in your class have disabilities similar to those covered in this guide? If they are not represented, can the activities be adapted to include those disabilities?

3. Look at your classroom layout. Is the classroom accessible? If not, what can you change to make it more accessible?

4. Can the curriculum activities in this guide be included as part of your regular schedule? When would be the best time for large-group activities, small-group activities?

Second, go through the Checklist for an Inclusive Environment. Looking at your answers, decide which areas in your room are inclusive and those where work is needed. Which of the activities best fit your classroom needs?

Third, go through the Annotated Bibliography in the Resources section. Which resources best fit your classroom needs?

Last, develop an action plan. Make a list of the activities and resources you will need to make your classroom more inclusive. Then begin to implement the curriculum.

SEE WHAT CHANGED

After you have incorporated the activities into a regular part of your curriculum and have been using them for several months, complete the General Classroom Information sheet and the Checklist for an Inclusive Environment again. Compare your initial responses to your later responses. Did your answers change on the checklist? In what areas? In what areas are your answers still "no"? Is your classroom set up differently? Are the trips and topic areas more inclusive? Is your classroom accessible?

Talk to the children about disability. Has their knowledge increased? Has their behavior toward people with disabilities changed, e.g., less teasing, less over-helping, less use of words such as blind and retard as insults? Based on what you have learned, go back and see what changes might still need to be made.

GENERAL CLASSROOM INFORMATION

The Children

How many children are in the class? _____

What is their age range? _____

How many, if any, children with disabilities are in the class? _____
Describe the disabilities.

The Curriculum

What, if any, class trips are scheduled this year?

What topic areas, e.g., body parts, will be covered this year?

The Schedule

Describe a typical class day, including both required activities, such as
circle time, and free choice activities, such as dress up.

MORNING			AFTERNOON		
Activity	Free Choice	Required	Activity	Free Choice	Required
_____	_____	_____	_____	_____	_____
_____	_____	_____	_____	_____	_____
_____	_____	_____	_____	_____	_____
_____	_____	_____	_____	_____	_____
_____	_____	_____	_____	_____	_____

The Classroom

Separately, make a labeled layout of the classroom, including tables,
chairs, bookcases, steps, and the various activity centers.

CHECKLIST FOR AN INCLUSIVE ENVIRONMENT

Children's Books

In selecting books, do you

Yes   No

Review the pictures for nonstereotypic portrayals of:

____ ____ Sex roles, e.g., show women and girls in assertive roles, men and boys in nurturing roles?

____ ____ Race, e.g., show people of color in leadership roles?

____ ____ Disability, e.g., show people with disabilities in active and interactive roles?

____ ____ Review the text for offensive language, e.g., handicapped, crippled, and the generic "he"?

____ ____ Choose some books that have a female, a person of color, or a person who is disabled as the main character?

____ ____ Choose some books that have a disabled person as the main character?

____ ____ Choose books that depict people with disabilities expressing feelings and being independent, and active?

____ ____ Select stories that stress similarities rather than differences between disabled and nondisabled people?

Pictures and Posters

Do the pictures on the walls in your classroom

Yes   No

____ ____ Include a representative number of adults and children with disabilities?

____ ____ Depict people with a variety of disabilities?

____ ____ Show adults who are disabled in a variety of roles, such as parents, business owners, community workers, or leaders, teachers, etc.?

____ ____ Show adults and children with disabilities interacting with others who are not disabled?

____ ____ Show a variety of people from different racial/ethnic and socioeconomic backgrounds?

____ ____ Include women and men involved in nontraditional occupations?

____ ____ Show girls being active and boys expressing feelings?

Trips and Visitors

When planning trips and visits do you

Yes   No

_____ _____ Invite adults with disabilities to visit your class to talk about their work?

_____ _____ Invite diverse people who will provide children with a variety of nontraditional role models?

_____ _____ Include visiting a person who is disabled at her or his worksite?

_____ _____ Plan class trips about accessibility to include pointing out curb cuts, ramps, or elevators with Braille buttons?

_____ _____ Provide children with varied ways to experience their environment, e.g., touch, smell, sound, taste?

In general

Yes   No

_____ _____ Do you find ways to incorporate disability into classroom activities?

_____ _____ Do you take into account the varying skill levels of every child and plan so all children can equally participate in the activities?

_____ _____ Are the classroom materials selected to provide children with positive role models of women, people of color, and people with disabilities?

_____ _____ Can the materials in the classroom be used by all children? If not, can the materials be adapted so that all children will have equal access to them?

_____ _____ Does the classroom environment provide children with a positive view of themselves and others?

_____ _____ Does the dramatic play area offer opportunities to explore a variety of experiences with disability, e.g., child-size crutches, eyeglass frames, hearing aids?

_____ _____ Can the dramatic play area be changed to simulate a school, a store, an office, or other work site?

_____ _____ Are you careful to use language that does not convey stereotypes of sex, race, or disability?

_____ _____ Are children's biases and misconceptions addressed in a sensitive and meaningful way?

_____ _____ Are all children in the class represented in some way in the classroom environment?

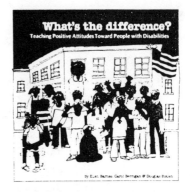

Resources

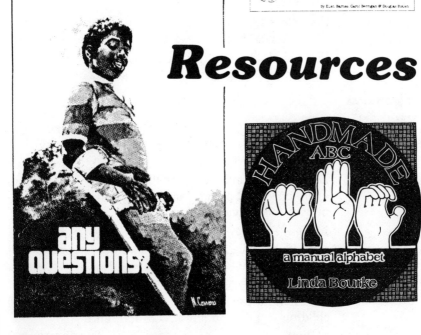

ANNOTATED BIBLIOGRAPHY:

Resources for Creating an Inclusive Classroom Environment

The following list of annotated resources will help to create an inclusive early childhood environment that is nonsexist and multicultural and includes images and active role models of adults and children with disabilities. The resources were assembled according to carefully predetermined criteria. An extensive search was conducted for books and materials that:

- Portray all characters in a nonsexist manner,
- Represent racial and ethnic diversity,
- Depict adults and children with disabilities in a positive light.

It is difficult to find materials and books that meet all these criteria simultaneously. Some of the books listed do not fulfill all the criteria, but they have redeeming qualities that make them worth noting. It is especially difficult to find books for young children that are written from the perspective of a child or adult with a disability. More often, a nondisabled character discusses the disability. For those titles that do not include people with disabilities, suggestions are given on how to extend the ideas and concepts to make the material become inclusive. The annotations reflect the positive aspects of each book and mention the drawbacks if any exist.

The bibliography is divided into the following categories: Curriculum Materials, Children's Books, Background Readings for Teachers and Parents, and Additional Resources. The double-starred entries designate items that are specifically recommended in the curriculum activities. Single-starred listings are those that have been suggested as alternatives within the activities. The Additional Resources section includes national disability organizations that have local chapters or affiliates as well as other groups that either have specific materials or can serve as sources of information, adaptive equipment, visitors, or volunteers.

Curriculum Materials

All About Me and Let's Be Friends: Book and Record Sets

Picture books and accompanying cassettes (or 45 rpm records) contain an original "Miss Jackie" song (sheet music on back page). The black-and-white photographs by David Giveans are nonsexist, multiracial, and inclusive of people with disabilities.

Gryphon House, Inc., 3706 Otis St., P.O. Box 275, Mt. Rainier, MD 20712. (800) 638-0928.

Everybody Is Somebody Special Coloring Book

A positive, nonsexist, and multiracial/ethnic book that is inclusive of people with disabilities. Its value lies in its text and illustrations rather than in its usefulness as a coloring book. *Developmental Disabilities Advocacy Network, Inc., 3540 North Progress Ave., Harrisburg, PA 17110. (717) 657-3320.*

Feeling Free Posters **

A set of three color posters includes: *If You Thought the Wheel Was a Good Idea, You'll Love the Ramp*, which features different views of ramps, with children on a variety of wheeled vehicles (including a wheel-chair) enjoying themselves; *We All Fit In,* which shows all kinds of children with disabilities interacting; and *Any Questions?* a picture of a boy on Canadian crutches. Also available is *Hi Friend,* a poster of a Dick Bruna drawing of one child pushing another in a wheelchair. *Human Policy Press, P.O. Box 127, Syracuse, NY 13210. (315) 423-3851.*

Handmade ABC: A Manual Alphabet *

This ABC book shows the manual alphabet (finger spell-

ing). A hand forming the letter sign is reproduced on one page, while a printed letter and several objects beginning with that letter are on the opposite page. Some of the objects representing the letters are not always appropriate for young children since they are either not clear or not within the experiences of a young child. Nevertheless, this is one of the easiest and clearest books available for learning finger spelling. Written by Linda Bourke. *Reading, MA: Addison Wesley Publishing Company, Inc., 1981. (617) 944-3700.*

Hospital Play Equipment *

A set of wooden hospital equipment, scaled 2 inches to 1 foot includes a wheelchair among other traditional hospital playthings. It is very important to separate hospital play from disability issues. Children should not be encouraged to think that people with disabilities are "sick." *Victor C. Dye, The Hospital Play Equipment Company, 1122 Judson Ave., Evanston, IL 60202. (312) 869-1888.*

Linda Bove, Actress **

This poster of Linda Bove, a member of the National Theatre of the Deaf and a regular cast member of *Sesame Street,* shows her signing "I love you." (The caption indicates a broader interpretation of the sign as "I like you.") Included is a biography of Linda Bove entitled "Breaking Down Barriers." *TABS: Aids for Ending Sexism in School, 744 Carroll St., Brooklyn, NY 11215. (718) 788-3478.*

New Friends **

This program includes a do-it-yourself pattern for making a child-size rag doll that can be adapted to depict several different disabilities. Also available are *New Friends Trainer's Notebook* and *New Friends Mainstreaming Activities To Help Young Children Understand and Accept Individual Differences.* The pattern is available separately from *The Chapel Hill Training Outreach Project, Lincoln Center, Merritt Hill Rd., Chapel Hill, NC 27514. (919) 967-8295.*

Resource Photos for Mainstreaming: Children and Adult Sets *

Two sets of black-and-white, 11 x 14 inch photographs provide children with positive role models of people with disabilities. The adult set shows people with disabilities in work, family, and recreational scenes; the children's set depicts children with disabilities in typical classroom activities. Also included in the children's set is a four-picture poster of an interracial family in which the mother is disabled. *Women's Action Alliance, Inc., 370 Lexington Ave., New York, NY 10017 (212) 532-8330.*

Sesame Street Sign Language Fun **

As the Muppets act out simple sentences, Linda Bove, a member of the National Theatre of the Deaf, illustrates the signs. Most illustrations are nonsexist, but some words are not, e.g., policeman. This is, however, the simplest sign language book around, and it is enjoyable. Produced by Children's Television Workshop. *New York: Random House/ Children's Television Workshop, 1980. (212) 572-2646.* Also available from *The National Association for the Deaf Bookstore, 814 Thayer Ave., Silver Springs, MD 20910. (301) 587-6282.*

Sign Blocks

A set of 1¼ inch alphabet blocks, printed with capital letters and the corresponding finger signs, are made of smooth wood and nontoxic paint. These blocks might be modified by making the letters tactile by covering them with glue and sand, adding Braille letters, or writing in lower-case letters for children who are more familiar with lower-case printing. *Diana Friedlander, Sign Blocks (A Division of U.S. Panel Products), 150 County Rd., Tenafly, NJ 07670. (201) 871-1900.*

Sign Language Clowns

In this coloring book, clowns act out 16 verbs that are also shown in American Sign Language and in the manual alphabet (with corresponding block letters). For pre-schoolers, the picture of the action and the sign for it can be used alone. For beginning readers, the manual alphabet and large letters can be added when appropriate. Each sign is on a separate page, and there are information and ideas on how to prepare and use the materials. The value of this material lies in its clear depiction of ASL rather than in its usefulness as a coloring book. Written by Ralph R. Miller Sr; clown illustrations by Betty G. Miller; sign illustrations by Frank Allen Paul. *(Berkeley, CA: Sign-Up Inc., 1984).* Distributed by *Gryphon House, 3706 Otis St., P.O. Box 275, Mount Rainier, MD 20712. (800) 638-0928.*

Special Friends *

A set of eight stuffed animals that have disabilities. Animals in the set include a monkey in a wheelchair, an elephant with a hearing aid, and a bear with a prosthesis for one leg. Produced by Pediatric Projects, Inc., P.O. Box 1880, Santa Monica, CA 90406. (213) 393-4260. Also available from *The Able Child, 325 West 11th St., New York, NY 10014. (212) 255-0068.*

Children's Books

About Handicaps: An Open Family Book for Parents and Children Together

This book combines a simple text about disabilities for children with an explanatory text for parents (or older children). The story deals with a nondisabled boy's fears as he encounters a child who has cerebral palsy and an adult with a prosthesis for an arm and hand. It also portrays the father's efforts to provide information to alleviate his son's fears. The story ends as the two children become friends. The book is not multiracial and features only males, but it is interesting and forthright and addresses important issues about disabilities in a unique format. Written by Sara Bonnett Stein with photographs by Dick Frank. *New York: Walker & Co., 1974; paperback edition, 1984.
(212) 265-3632.*

All Kinds of Families

All kinds of families doing all kinds of things are depicted in soft, warm, color drawings. Included in family scenes are a

boy in a wheelchair and an older person with a cane. Scenes of a funeral, a wedding, and a visit to a parent in jail are interspersed with picnic scenes, holiday scenes, and other traditional family activities. Nonsexist and multiracial. Written by Norma Simon and illustrated by Joe Lasker. *Chicago: Albert Whitman & Co., 1976. (312) 647-1355.*

The Balancing Girl

This is a story about a girl who uses a wheelchair and is mainstreamed into a first-grade class. The story tells about the many things the girl can do and her particular talent for balancing all kinds of objects. A serious drawback is the fact that this book is not multiracial.

This requires some thought before putting it in a classroom library, but the child is portrayed in such a positive light that it is worth noting here. Written by Bernice Rabe and illustrated by Lillian Hoban. *New York: E.P. Dutton, 1981. (212) 725-1818.*

Bodies **

This book presents a good way to begin thinking about human bodies and how they work. It is multiracial and nonsexist. Although it is not inclusive of people with disabilities, since it discusses body parts and functions, it can be used to introduce disability. Written by Barbara Brenner with photographs by George Ancona. *New York: E.P. Dutton, 1973. (212) 725-1818.*

A Button in Her Ear *

Angela, who is hearing impaired, describes how she misinterprets what she hears until she gets a hearing aid. When her parents take her to the doctor, he refers them to a hearing specialist who is a Black woman. Angela plays baseball and is friends with boys and girls. The softly-colored and black-and-white illustrations are multiracial. Written by Ada B. Litchfield and illustrated by Eleanor Mill. *Chicago: Albert Whitman & Co., 1976. (312) 647-1355.*

A Cane In Her Hand *

Valerie, who is visually impaired, describes how she learns to use a long cane so she won't bump into things any more. Readers join Valerie at her visit to the eye doctor, in school, where her teacher is helpful and supportive, and with her friends both male and female. Since *A Cane in Her Hand* is for older readers, it may be appropriate to paraphrase some of the text for younger children. Written by

Ada B. Litchfield and illustrated by Eleanor Mill. *Chicago: Albert Whitman & Co., 1977. (312) 647-1355.*

Danny's Song **

A book about a boy on crutches that stresses the many things he does well and deals with his frustrations caused by having to do some things more slowly. This book is part of the "I Am, I Can, I Will" set of materials created by Mr. Rogers, but it is available separately if ordered by an individual. Written by Betsy P. Nadas and designed by Frank Dastolfo and William Panos. *Northbrook, IL: Hubbard, 1975. (800) 323-8368.*

Darlene **
A little girl named Darlene, who uses a wheelchair, is feeling homesick while spending a morning with her uncle and cousin. Darlene resists her cousin's attempts to play with her, but finally becomes absorbed in games and in her uncle's guitar playing. In typical fashion, when Darlene's mother arrives, Darlene doesn't want to go home. *Darlene* is outstanding because the child's disability is secondary to the plot, it portrays a Black family, and has a male caregiver as a main character. Written by Eloise Greenfield and illustrated by George Ford. *New York: Methuen, 1980. (212) 922-3550.*

Good Morning Franny, Good Night Franny
Franny is a lively youngster who enjoys "zipping" around in her wheelchair. Ting is Franny's friend. The two girls have many adventures together in the park. Colorful, multiracial pictures add a great deal to this story. There is one objection to the text. Ting either "takes" or "sneaks" toys from the family's store for her and Franny to play with. Several important issues are touched upon—disability, hospitalization, and friendship. Written by Emily Hearn and illustrated by Mark Thurman. *Toronto: Canada Women's Press, 1984. (416) 598-0082.*

Grandma's Wheelchair
This story is about the warm relationship between grandma and her four-year-old grandson, Nat. Grandma uses a wheelchair, and Nat spends a lot of time riding in her lap while they do things together. Grandma is depicted as a homemaker and is portrayed as being capable and taking an active role in the running of the home. Information regarding wheelchair use is an integral

part of the story. Written by Lorraine Henriod and illustrated by Christa Chevalier. *Chicago: Albert Whitman & Co., 1982. (312) 647-1355.*

Grown-Ups Cry Too

A story that depicts a wide range of emotions—sadness, anger, fatigue, fear, and happiness as expressed with tears —in Stanley Kramer's family. Stanley explains the reasons why a baby cries, relates experiences that made him cry, and tells about many different situations in which his mother and/or father and grandmother cried, too. This nonsexist, multiracial book is not inclusive of people with disabilities, but it is a good story to stimulate discussions about emotions. Written and illustrated by Nancy Hazen. *Chapel Hill, NC: Lollipop Power, 1973. (919) 929-4857.*

He's My Brother

The story of Jamie, who is developmentally disabled, as told by his brother, balances the things Jamie can do well with the things he does more slowly. It deals with the frustration, hurt, and anger that Jamie experiences, as well as the joys he feels. A combination of softly-colored and black-and-white illustrations sets a contemporary but gentle tone for this realistic, nonsexist, and multiracial book. Written and illustrated by Joe Lasker. *Chicago: Albert Whitman & Co., 1974. (312) 647-1355.*

Howie Helps Himself

This was one of the first books that addressed the subject of a child who is severely disabled learning and succeeding. The

multiracial and nonsexist illustrations depict girls and boys "zooming" around in their wheelchairs. Howie's father is portrayed as a very nurturing person. There is also an excellent picture of an accessible school bus. However, adults may want to read the text selectively to create a better balance between what Howie can do and what he can't do. Written by Joan Fassler and illustrated by Joe Lasker. *Chicago: Albert Whitman & Co., 1975. (312) 647-1355.*

I Have a Sister, My Sister Is Deaf *

This story talks about what it is like to have a sister who is deaf and provides information about how she communicates with her family and friends. The sisters are shown doing many things together. There is a good balance between what the girl who is deaf can and can't do. The phrase "I have a Sister" is repeated many times and makes reading somewhat choppy. It may be helpful to paraphrase. Written by Jeanne Whitehouse Peterson and illustrated by Debora Ray. *New York: Harper & Row, 1977; paperback edition, 1984. (800) 242-7737.*

Jo, Flo and Yolanda

This is a delightful nonsexist story about triplets. It describes the ways the girls are the same as well as the many ways they are different. Although not inclusive of people with disabilities, it is an excellent way to begin a discussion about the similarities and differences among people. It

depicts a Hispanic family and is set in a multiracial neighborhood. Written by Carol dePoix and illustrated by Stephanie Sove Ney. *Chapel Hill, NC: Lollipop Power, 1973. (919) 929-4857.*

My Favorite Place **

This story is full of the multisensory experiences of a child's trip to the ocean. It is not until the end that the reader finds out that the girl is blind. *My Favorite Place* helps young children understand the use of the senses other than vision —hearing, touch, smell, and taste. The child is shown actively swimming in the ocean and running from the waves. Written by Susan Sargent and Donna Aaron Wirt and illustrated by Allan Eitzen. *Nashville: Abingdon Press, 1983. (615) 749-6347.*

My Friend Jacob

The story of two friends—an eight-year-old boy, Sam, and his seventeen-year-old friend, Jacob, who is mentally retarded—focuses on the friendship, the activities the boys share, and the things they do for each other. The multiracial illustrations are soft black-and-white sketches. Written by Lucille Clifton and illustrated by Thomas DiGrazia. *New York: E.P. Dutton, 1980. (212) 725-1818.*

My Friend Leslie

Karen tells us about her friend Leslie, a classmate who has multiple disabilities. The story describes a typical day in school, including all the activities that Leslie, Karen, and the other children do. Leslie is shown working independently as well as accepting assistance from her peers. Accommodations are made to enable Leslie to participate fully. *My Friend Leslie* is a realistic portrayal of a successful mainstreaming effort. It would be appropriate to use in a classroom discussion of a variety of disabilities. Written by Maxine B. Rosenberg with photographs by George Ancona. *New York: Lothrop, Lee & Shepard, 1983. (212) 889-3050.*

Roly Goes Exploring **

A simple shapes story with cut-out "pictures" to feel as well as to see. The text is in both Braille and print and can be shared and enjoyed by sighted and blind children. Roly is a circle that is referred to as "he." To make the story nonsexist, adult readers can alternate using she or he or it. With this modification, it is an excellent book for children. Written by Philip Newth. *New York: Philomel Books, 1981. (212) 689-9200.*

Through Grandpa's Eyes

In this sensitive story about a boy and his grandfather, readers learn a great deal about how grandpa, who is blind, does many things. The relationship between grandpa and John is a warm and loving one. Grandpa teaches John to use all his senses to appreciate his environment. Both grandmother and grandfather are depicted as active, functioning people. It is a pity that grandpa is never shown with any kind of mobility aid such as a cane or guide dog. Also his sense of smell seems almost too good to be true. Despite this, *Through Grandpa's Eyes* provides a positive portrayal of an adult who is blind. Written by Patricia MacLachlan and illustrated by Deborah Ray. *New York: Harper & Row, 1980. (800) 242-7737.*

Touch Me Book *

The *Touch Me Book*, a Golden Touch and Feel Book, is a natural for a discussion of how things feel. There are many good examples of textures that children like to touch, including soft fur, smooth plastic, and sticky tape. Teachers may want to see how many of the things mentioned in the book are readily available at their school or center. Written by Pat and Eve Witte and illustrated by Harlow Rockwell. *Racine, WI: Western Publishing Company, 1961. (414) 633-2431.*

Who Am I? **

This book portrays a little girl who is hearing impaired playing, loving her family, and learning. The title words, "Who Am I" are the only words in the book, and they appear periodically throughout the text. The photo illustrations are full color, nonsexist, multiracial, and inclusive. The book is part of a comprehensive set of books, audio cassettes, video tapes, and films entitled, "I Am, I Can, I Will," by Mr. Rogers, but it is available separately if ordered by an individual. Written by Barry Head and Jim Seguin. Designed by Frank Dastolfo and photographed by Walter Seng. *Northbrook, IL: Hubbard, 1975. (800) 323-8368.*

Why Am I Different? **

Although this book does not include people with disabilities, it is an excellent way to begin a discussion of how all people are the same and how they are all different. The book is non-sexist, multicultural, and depicts people of varying ages active in the community. It is unfortunate that one of the first pictures of a difference shows a boy bigger than a girl. Also, the black-and-white pictures make the differences in hair color unclear for young children. Written by Norma Simon and illustrated by Dora Leder. *Chicago: Albert Whitman & Co., 1976. (312) 647-1355.*

Words in Our Hands

This unusual story about three children whose parents are deaf discusses finger spelling, sign language, speech, and lip reading. It deals realistically with the family's move to a new town and with the increased unease the children feel because their parents are deaf. This is a long, involved book for young children and probably needs to be "talked." Written by Ada B. Litchfield and illustrated by Helen Cogan Cherry. *Chicago: Albert Whitman & Co., 1980. (312) 647-1355.*

Background Readings for Teachers and Parents

Barrier Awareness Series

This series of pamphlets is an excellent resource for information about disability and awareness training. The series includes "The Invisible Barrier," "Free Wheeling," "Sense Ability," "Inside Out," "Perspectives," "Overdue Process: Providing Legal Services to Disabled Clients," "Partners," "Getting Together," and "Fair Play." *Regional Rehabilitation Research Institute on Attitudinal, Legal, and Leisure Barriers, George Washington University, Academic Center, Suite T-605, 801 22nd St., NW Washington, D.C. 20052. (202) 676-6377.*

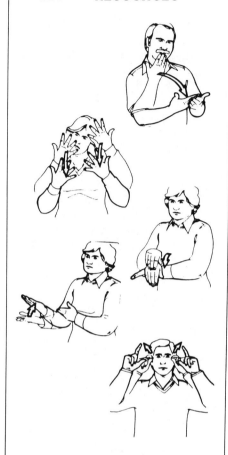

Basic Sign Communication: Vocabulary

This sign language dictionary includes basic adult conversational communication. The vocabulary section is the first of three sections. The signs are clear and are represented by women and men who are themselves deaf. The format is not meant for children, but it is possible to make copies of the signs for presentation in your classroom. Written by William J. Newell and illustrated by Frank Allen Paul. *Silver Spring, MD: National Association of the Deaf, 1983. (301) 587-6282.*

Books for Today's Children

This annotated bibliography of picture books focuses on good books for children that avoid stereotyped attitudes. There are stories that feature active girls and gentle boys, that show children living in a variety of cultures and family structures, and that include the experience of disability. Compiled by Jeanne Bracken and Sharon Wigutoff. *Old Westbury, NY: Feminist Press, 1979. (516) 876-3086.*

Bulletin

Several issues of this newsletter provide excellent resources for creating an inclusive classroom environment. Volume 8, numbers 6 and 7, 1977, are a special issue on handicapism and how it is reinforced in children's books and other media. Volume 13, numbers 4 and 5, 1982, are devoted to a five-year update on handicapism in children's books, including an updated criteria for

Handicapism in Children's Books:
A Five-Year Update

selecting nonhandicapist materials. Volume 14, numbers 7 and 8, 1983, is a special double issue on early childhood education. The article "Providing an Anti-Handicapist Early Childhood Environment" makes links between sexism, racism, and handicapism and contains suggestions for creating an inclusive early childhood classroom. Volume 11, numbers 3 and 4, 1980, is devoted to "Children, Race and Racism: How Race Awareness Develops." *Council on Interracial Books for Children, Inc., 1841 Broadway, New York, NY 10023. (212) 757-5339.*

Creating Inclusive Non-stereotyping Environments: The Child with a Disability

Issues of sex and disability bias in the early childhood classroom are explored. Parallels are drawn between the effects of sexist and handicapist attitudes on children with and without disabilites. Disabled girls and boys are "feminized" in the most traditional and negative way. This in turn thrusts disabled children into care-receiving roles rather than care-giving roles. The child with a disability is restricted by too much or indiscriminate assistance. Such limiting deprives children of the opportunity to develop skills and competencies. Written by Mary Ann Lang PhD. (unpublished manuscript). For a copy, send $1 to *Educational Equity Concepts, Inc., 440 Park Ave. South, New York, NY 10016. (212) 725-1803.*

Disabled Women: The Case of the Missing Role Model

In this thought-provoking article, the author makes the connections between sex, race/ethnicity, and disability bias. The personal anecdotes help the reader to understand clearly the discrimination experienced by women with disabilities. The article discusses the issues of housing, employment and poverty, health care, and family planning. Written by Katherine Corbett in *Independent, issue 2, 1979.* For a reprint, send $1 to *Educational Equity Concepts, Inc., 440 Park Ave. South, New York, NY 10016. (212) 725-1803.*

A Difference in the Family

This book, written specifically for families with a child who is disabled, tries to cover the practical and emotional aspects of the situation. The author is herself the parent of a child with a disability, and this gives the text authenticity. There is a genuine effort to avoid sexist language—parents usually means mother and/or father, and the generic "he" does not prevail, although there are some lapses. Written by Helen Featherstone. *New York: Basic Books, 1980. (800) 242-7737.*

Equal Play

Three issues of this newsletter are devoted to a discussion of mainstreaming and an inclusive early childhood classroom environment: Volume I, number 1, winter 1980, "Mainstreaming Children"; volume II, numbers 1 and 2, winter/spring, 1981, "Creating a New Mainstream"; and volume III, numbers 1 and 2, winter/spring 1982, "Access to Equality." *Women's Action Alliance, Inc., 370 Lexington Ave., New York, NY 10017. (212) 532-8330.*

Exceptional Parent Magazine

This outstanding periodical provides information and support for parents of children with disabilities. It is an excellent resource for anyone who is interested in issues of disability from a parent's point of view. A "Directory of Organizations and Agencies Serving Children and Adults with Disabilities and Their Families" is included in the August 1984 issue (volume 14). The directory is available separately for $1. *Exceptional Parent Magazine, 605 Commonwealth Ave., Boston, MA 02215. (617) 536-8961.*

Like It Is: Facts and Feelings About Handicaps from Kids Who Know

Girls and boys discuss their disabilites, which include hearing impairment, visual impairment, orthopedic impairment, developmental disability, mental retardation, learning disability, and behavioral disorders, in an open, frank manner. They talk about the wide range of impairments that fall into each of the above categories. The people with disabilities are shown participating in many varied activities. This book is for adults as well as elementary school children who are good readers. The material about disability is presented in an informative, interesting way. A serious drawback is the use of the word "handicapped" throughout the text rather than "disabled" or "disability." Written by Barbara Adams with photographs by James Stanfield. *New York: Walker and Co., 1979. (212) 265-3632.*

Mainstreaming: Ideas for Teaching Young Children

This approach to mainstreaming conveys respect for children and parents throughout and is based on a program developed by the Early Education Center of the Amherst-Pelham Public Schools in Massachusetts. The text speaks of the "special" and "regular" needs of children and uses the words "child" and "children" followed by actual female and male examples and illustrations. Filled with practical ideas about developing Individual Education Plans, classroom management, and curriculum, the book conveys a positive and humane view of behavior management. Written by Judith Souweine, Sheila Crimmins, and Carolyn Mazel (1981). *National Association for the Education of Young Children, 1834 Connecticut Ave., NW, Washington, DC 20009. (202) 232-8777.*

Mainstreaming in Early Childhood Education

This is a basic book about mainstreaming that covers causes of disabilities, legislation, teaching, curriculum, management, and working with the home and community. The pictures of children and adults interspersed throughout are multiracial/ethnic, and the children are interactive, not isolated. Written by K. Eileen Allen. *Albany, NY: Delmar Publisher, 1980. (518) 459-1150.*

No More Stares

A landmark book that provides postive role models of women with disabilities. The excellent and sensitive black-and-white photographs show women with disabilities in action: working on the job, at home, and at school; participating in sports; with children, colleagues, and friends or family. It also contains an extensive resource bibliography. Conceived and developed by Ann Cupolo Carrillo, Katherine Corbett, and Victoria Lewis (1982). Available in print and on tape from *The Disability Rights Education and Defense Fund, 2032 San Pablo Ave., Berkeley, CA 94702. (800) 227-2472.*

Non-Sexist Education for Young Children: A Practical Guide

This first curriculum for nonsexist early childhood education contains practical,

how-to approaches and ideas and includes a "Checklist for a Non-Sexist Classroom." The book is full of anecdotes from teachers, children, and parents. Written by Barbara Sprung (New York: Citation Press, 1975). Available from *Educational Equity Concepts, Inc., 440 Park Ave. South, New York NY 10016. (212) 725-1803.*

Project Head Start: Mainstreaming Preschoolers

Each book in this series of eight manuals for teachers, parents, and others who work with disabled preschoolers addresses a different impairment —hearing, visual, orthopedic, mental retardation, health, emotional, learning disabilities, and language. The manuals are informative and easy to read and understand. They are also available in Spanish. The language is nonsexist, and the children and adults depicted are multiracial/ethnic. For more information, contact your local *Resource Access Project* or *Publications, Head Start Bureau, Administration for Children, Youth and Families, Washington, DC 20024. (202) 755-7782.*

Talking: Between the Lines

This training guide, a workshop series on communicating with children in early childhood settings, was developed to help examine children's questions about disability. Its overall objective is to foster understanding of some of the skills needed to communicate with young children and specifically for developing sensitivity to language usage and individual children's needs. The guide provides training materials (including tapes) and a resource list. Written by Judith Rothschild-Stolberg, Michelle Rutman, and Dinah Heller. (New York: New York Universi-ty, 1983). For information contact *New York University Resource Access Project, 3 Washington Square Village, Suite 1M, New York, NY 10012. (212) 598-2144.*

The Unexpected Minority: Handicapped Children in America

This is a seminal book about issues of disability in contemporary America. Exclusion, the often excessive focus on a child's disability (the "medical model"), rather than on the whole child and possibilities for far greater options are all discussed. There is, however, a major flaw in this otherwise fine book—the generic "he" is used throughout, which symbolizes a lack of sensitivity on the part of the authors to issues of sex roles. Although this is a very serious lapse, especially for a 1980 publication, in every other respect the book is excellent, and there is nothing else that addresses issues of disability so comprehensively. According to the publisher, the book is temporarily out of print but can still be found in libraries. Written by John Gliedman and William Roth. *New York: Harcourt, Brace, Jovanovich, 1980. (800) 543-1918.*

What If You Couldn't. . . ?
This informative, simply written book, which provides basic information about what it is like to be disabled, is interesting both for adults as well as for elementary school children who are good readers. The drawings show a variety of active children and adults with disabilities. Written by Janet Kamien and illustrated by Signe Hanson. *New York: Charles Scribner's Sons, 1979. (800) 257-5755.*

**What's the Difference?
Teaching Positive Attitudes
toward People with
Disabilities**
This curriculum guide provides information on a variety of disabilities including health impairments, hearing impairments, learning disabilities, motor impairments, mental retardation, speech and

language impairments, visual impairments, and emotional disturbances. There are many activities for elementary school children that are designed to increase children's awareness of and sensitivity to people with disabilities. There are in-depth discussions of the causes and effects of negative attitudes leading to discrimination and how to begin to change and eliminate them. *What's the Difference?* can help expand the curriculum into many areas of disability. The information and activities can be modified for younger children. Written by Ellen Barnes, Carol Berrigan, and Douglas Biklen. *Syracuse, NY: Human Policy Press, 1978. (315) 423-3851.*

Additional Resources

American Brotherhood for the Blind *

This organization has a lending library of children's books that are both in print and in Braille. It is a free service, and teachers will be accommodated whenever possible. Unfortunately, there is no catalog from which to choose titles. If you wish to order a book, it is a good idea to request several specific titles and/or provide the age level and interest area of your class. When you receive a book, be sure that it is nonsexist and multiracial—do not put a book in your classroom library just because it is in Braille. *American Brotherhood for the Blind, Twin Vision Books, 18440 Oxnard St., Tarzana, CA 91356. (213) 343-2022.*

American Foundation for the Blind

A national organization that deals with all aspects of visual impairment. Pamphlets are available on request (single copies free) on such topics as "What to do when you meet a blind person" and "Understanding Braille." Unfortunately, the generic "he" is used, but otherwise the information is informative and accurate. A "Directory of Agencies Serving the Blind and Visually Handicapped" also is available as are single copies of alphabet cards in Braille and a pamphlet on deaf/blindness, which includes the one-handed manual alphabet. The AFB also may be helpful in locating a rehabilitation or education program in your local area. It is from these community resources that you may find a Braille print book to borrow as well as long canes that are not being used and can be cut down to child size. This may be one way to locate a person who is blind who would visit your classroom. There are five regional offices: San Francisco, Denver, Chicago, Atlanta, and Washington, DC. *American Foundation for the Blind, 15 West 16th St., New York, NY 10011. (212) 620-2000.*

Association on Handicapped Student Service Programs in Post-Secondary Education (AHSSPPE)

This is a national association of disabled student service coordinators at the postsecondary level. Service providers—many of whom are disabled—as well as college students with disabilities may be available to visit your school or center. Call the phone number for a directory/listing of disabled student service programs and contact people in your geographical area. AHSSPPE is most interested in bridging the gap between elementary, secondary, and postsecondary disabled student services. *AHSSPPE, P.O. Box 21192, Columbus, OH 43221. (614) 488-4972 (voice and TTY).*

Educational Equity Concepts, Inc.
A national, nonprofit organization founded in 1983 to create educational programs and materials that are free of sex, race, and disability bias. The organization also offers training programs for parents, students, teachers, and other professionals and engages in a variety of public education activities fostering excellence and equity. Current early childhood programs emphasize math, science, and mainstreaming and the development of classroom resources such as puppets, block accessories, and curriculum guides. Other resources include a video tape of a speakout in support of equity in educational programs and a manual for workshop leaders working to raise awareness of issues of women and disability. *Educational Equity Concepts, Inc., 440 Park Ave. South, New York, NY 10016. (212) 725-1803.*

Educators with Disabilities: A Resource Guide
This directory includes profiles of educators with disabilities (ten categories) as well as recommendations about barriers faced by educators with disabilities. The directory is nationwide and is arranged by disability area, geographical area, and teaching specialty (Washington, DC: American Association of Colleges for Teacher Education, 1981). *Superintendent of Documents, U.S. Government Printing Office, Washington, DC. 20402 (202) 783-3238.*

The 52 Association *
This organization's main focus is rehabilitation through sports. Pictures of people with disabilities participating in sports activities are available free of charge upon request. The photographs are black and white with some advertising on the bottom that can be cut off for display in the classroom. There is also a newsletter, *Confidence Through Sports,* which has pictures of people with disabilities involved in sports. In volume 2, Ski Issue, winter 1983/84, there are photographs of a skier who is disabled and a basketball player in a wheelchair. There are more pictures of men than women; therefore, choose your display materials carefully so that males and females are equally represented. *The 52 Association, Inc., 441 Lexington Ave., New York, NY 10017. (800) 367-6768.*

Gallaudet College for the Deaf

The College issues a listing of various organizations and programs serving people who are hearing impaired throughout the United States. From this list you may find hearing aid dealers and/or a volunteer who is hearing impaired who would come and visit your classroom. *Gallaudet College for the Deaf, Office of Public Relations, Kendall Green, T-6, Washington, DC 20002. (202) 651-5591 (voice and TTY).*

Gryphon House, Inc.

Gryphon House is committed to supplying educators with nonsexist, multiracial, and, more recently, books that are inclusive of people with disabilities. It has a comprehensive collection of quality books for children and teachers.

 gryphon house

Howe Press *

The Howe Press has a variety of equipment and devices that aid people who are partially sighted or blind to write (both in print and in Braille) and draw with raised lines. In addition, the Howe Press has a limited number of books that are available in both print and Braille, e.g., some of the Golden Books, the Scratch and Sniff series, and *The Little Engine That Could.* This kind of book is a must if there is a child who is blind in your classroom. It makes it possible for all children (sighted and blind) as well as visually impaired teachers and parents to share the same story. A catalog of titles is available. Howe Press, *Perkins School for the Blind, 175 North Beacon St., Watertown, MA 02172. (617) 924-3434.*

Kids on the Block

This puppet education program is designed to teach children about a variety of disabilities. Puppeteers trained by the project bring 3½-foot puppets. to schools and present shows that feature people with disabilities at work and play. The audience participates by engaging in dialogues with the puppets which were created by Barbara Aiello, a special education teacher. The puppets originated in Washington, DC, as "The Kids on the Block." Many school systems across the nation have the program. *Kids on the Block, 822 North Fairfax St., Alexandria, VA 22314. (800) 368-5437* or *The Kids' Project, New York State Office of Mental Retardation and Developmental Disabilities, 44 Holland Ave., Albany, NY 12229. (518) 473-3500.*

The KIDS Project, Inc.

In this project, KIDS stands for Keys to Introducing Disability in Society. This training program, staffed by people, both disabled and nondisabled, offers awareness training about disabilities to school personnel and children from kindergarten through sixth grade. Current work involves training teams of disabled and nondisabled people to implement the disability awareness curricula formerly developed by the Project. The Project sells a resource guide and a coloring book featuring people with disabilities in everyday situations. *KIDS Project, Inc., The Berkeley Model Mainstreaming School, 2955 Claremont Ave., Berkeley, CA 94705. (415) 848-5234.*

Library of Congress *

The Library of Congress maintains 140 regional libraries throughout the United States. Some regional libraries will lend Braille books to teachers for limited periods of time. If not, the branch in your area may have information on an alternate source such as a local program for people with visual impairments. The Library of Congress also distributes Braille alphabet sheets in unlimited quantities. This is a page of Braille paper with the raised Braille dots and corresponding print letters. It also includes numbers and punctuation marks. To find the location of the library in your state, contact the *Library of Congress, Division for the Blind and Physically Handicapped, Washington, DC 20542. (202) 287-5100.*

Local Merchants **

Local merchants who sell glasses or hearing aids often are willing to make contributions of glasses both with and without lenses and hearing aids both working and not. It is more difficult, however, to obtain wheelchairs, braces, or walkers. Surgical supply companies are good places to begin looking, and hospital physical therapy departments and nursing homes also may be willing to give away equipment they no longer use. Volunteer ambulance companies, too, may be a resource for wheelchair loans. Local rehabilitation centers and schools for people who are deaf, blind, or orthopedically impaired are other sources for fiberglass canes, hearing aids, glasses, wheelchairs, helmets, and walkers. Finally, airlines provide wheelchairs when necessary for travelers who are disabled. It may be possible to borrow a wheelchair for a limited time from a local airline.

National Association for Hearing and Speech Action

This is the consumer branch of the American Speech and Hearing Association. It will send a single copy of the manual alphabet (finger spelling) on request. In addition, it will supply local information regarding acquisition of hearing aids. *National Association for Hearing and Speech Action, 10801 Rockville Pike, Rockville, MD 20852. (800) 638-8255 (voice and TTY).*

National Association for the Deaf *

This organization has affiliates throughout the United States. It will provide several informative pamphlets on hearing impairment and what the organization does. It also has a book store with a variety of materials relating to deafness and hearing impairment. Call or write for pamphlets and a book store catalog as well as for local information about hearing aids and volunteer visitors. *National Association for the Deaf, 814 Thayer Ave., Silver Springs, MD 20910. (301) 587-1788 (office, voice and TTY); (301) 587-6282 (bookstore, voice and TTY).*

National Easter Seal Society

This organization provides information that may be helpful when you are considering accessibility. Its pamphlet, "Taking Down the Barriers," is an excellent resource and is free on request. The Society has a program of lending equipment to people with disabilities, and it may be possible to borrow a variety of devices, including wheelchairs, walkers, or braces. *National Easter Seal Society, 2023 West Ogden Ave., Chicago, IL 60612. (312) 243-8400.*

Office for Civil Rights, Office for Special Concerns

A packet of materials on Section 504 is available on request. The packet includes regulations, several brochures, and a fact sheet. The Office for Civil Rights also maintains a Section 504 Technical Assistance staff at each of ten regional offices. For information contact *U.S. Department of Education, 330 C St. S.W., Room 5116, Washington, DC 20202. (202) 245-0015.*

President's Committee on the Employment of the Handicapped

Through this government office it is possible to obtain a listing of state offices on advocacy for the disabled. Request a copy of the "State Chairmen and Secretaries List" to find the office of advocacy in your state. *President's Committee on the Employment of the Handicapped, 1111 20th St. N.W., Room 614, Washington, DC 20036. (202) 653-5153.*

Resource Access Projects (RAPS)

There are fifteen RAPS located in the ten federal regions across the country. As resources for the Head Start mainstreaming effort, RAPS provide training, technical assistance, and resources. For information about where the RAP is in your region, contact the *Administration for Children, Youth and Families, Head Start Bureau, Washington, DC. 20024. (202) 755-7710.*

Sports and Spokes **
This magazine provides information on wheelchair sports and recreation. Multiracial photographs of athletes (adults and children) who use wheelchairs are available for purchase or loan. *Sports and Spokes, 5201 North 19 Ave., Suite 111, Phoenix, AZ 85015. (602) 246-9426.*

State and Local Departments
Each state has its own Department of Education located, as a rule, in the state capitol. If you are looking for information regarding any disability, your State Education Department will provide information about services available. State Advocates for the Disabled (see President's Committee on Employment of the Handicapped) and Mayors' Offices for the Handicapped also are sources of information and services.

W.F.R./Aqua-Plast
This material is marvelous for molding a plastic brace for any size doll (or person, for that matter). The plastic can be molded by submerging it in hot water and then shaping it to fit the doll. It is a good idea to try to mold a small piece before submerging the entire piece in hot water so you get a sense of the material's properties. *W.F.R./Aqua-Plast, P.O. Box 215, Ramsey, NJ 07446. (800) 526-5247.*

INFORMATION ABOUT DISABILITY

HEARING IMPAIRMENT

There are approximately 16.7 million people in the United States today with hearing impairments ranging from mild to profound. Of these, three million are school-aged children. A person who is mildly to moderately hearing impaired is someone whose hearing does not preclude the understanding of speech through the ear alone, with or without a hearing aid. A person who is severely to profoundly hearing impaired is someone whose hearing does preclude the understanding of speech through the ear alone, with or without the use of a hearing aid.

People who are hearing impaired may use a hearing aid that amplifies all sounds. This takes time to become used to, and in a noisy place it may be overwhelming. Most hearing aids are small and fit in or around a person's ear(s). Some hearing aids are attached by a cord to a battery pack, which fits in a pocket or for a young child in a special harness on the chest. For some people a hearing aid is placed in both ears. This is called a bilateral or bineural hearing aid.

There are many ways that people with hearing impairments communicate. There are several methods of talking without the voice: American Sign Language (ASL), signed English, and finger spelling. In ASL a sign is made with one or two hands for each word or idea. There are more than 500,000 signs in ASL, and it is used by hundreds of thousands of people throughout the United States.

ASL is a language in and of itself. Signed English is a word-for-word translation of spoken English into signs. In finger spelling, which uses the manual alphabet, words are formed letter by letter with the fingers of one hand.

Another method of communication is the oral method in which children learn through speech reading (lip reading) and an amplification of sound. Speech is used, and signs are prohibited.

Total communication is a philosophy in which full communication is established through the employment of one or a combination of the above methods, whatever is the most effective for the persons involved in the give and take of communication. These methods include ASL, finger spelling, signed English, lip reading, writing, reading, body movements, and facial expression.

There are some devices that aid people with hearing impairments. One device is a system of lights that flash when an alarm clock, doorbell, or telephone rings. Another device is a TTY, which enables a person to type a conversation over the telephone rather than speaking it. The person being called receives the typed message on her or his machine. It is necessary for both participants in a conversation to have a TTY.

Barnes, Ellen, Berrigan, Carol, and Biklen, Douglas. *What's the Difference: Teaching Positive Attitudes Toward People with Disabilities,* Syracuse, NY: Human Policy Press, 1978.

Beyond the Sound Barrier. From Regional Rehabilitation Research Institute on Attitudinal, Legal, and Leisure Barriers, 1828 L. St., N.W., Suite 704, Washington, DC 20036.

Kamien, Janet. *What If You Couldn't...? A Book About Special Needs,* New York: Charles Scribner's Sons, 1979.

Kids on the Block. From State of New York Office of Mental Retardation and Development Disabilities, 44 Holland Ave., Albany, NY 12229.

Mainstreaming Preschoolers: Children with Hearing Impairment. From Project Head Start, U.S. Department of Health, Education and Welfare, DHEW Publication No. (OHDS) 78-31116.

Statistics from *Beyond the Sound Barrier.*

VISUAL IMPAIRMENT

A national health interview survey indicates that approximately 11.4 million people in the United States have some visual impairment even with glasses. Of these, 75,000 are children. There is a broad range of visual impairment. It includes people who can see at 20 feet, with best correction, what people with unimpaired vision can see at 70 to 199 feet. It also includes people who can see at 20 feet or less, with best correction, what people with unimpaired vision can see at 200 feet or more. A person with a visual impairment may also have a restricted visual field of 20 degrees or less. This is known as tunnel vision. A person with total loss of visual image, although light and shadows may be perceived, is defined as blind.

Wearing corrective lenses (glasses) may improve some people's less-than-average vision. Lenses are a device for forming an image of an object by refraction of light. Corrective lenses are made by polishing glass to make the surface concave or convex. Plastic lenses are made from a mold rather than by polishing and produce the same results as glass lenses.

For a person with a visual impairment for whom glasses may help little or not at all, there are many other reading aids: tape recorders, recorded books, large-print materials, magnifying glasses, and other devices such as the monocular, which is something like a telescope.

Braille is a system that enables people to read by running their fingers over raised dots. Braille is made from combinations of six dots, which form letters, words, numbers, and punctuation marks. It is possible to write Braille by using a machine called a Braille writer, an electric Braille typewriter, or a slate and stylus.

The mobility options most commonly used by persons with visual impairments are sighted guides, canes, and guide dogs. The person with a visual impairment holds the elbow of a sighted guide, and they walk together. A cane is usually called a long cane, a white cane, or a prescription cane. Its length is determined by the individual user's height and length of stride. The cane is moved in an arc in front of the user so that obstacles may be detected by it. Canes are traditionally white with a red tip. They are the most common means of independent travel for persons who are blind. Children can be taught to use a cane as early as they are ready to travel independently, as a rule about age 9 or 10. People who are over age 18 may choose to learn to use a guide dog. These dogs are carefully selected and trained in special schools before they are matched with their owners.

Barnes, Ellen, Berrigan, Carol, and Biklen, Douglas. *What's the Difference: Teaching Positive Attitudes Toward People with Disabilities,* Syracuse, NY: Human Policy Press, 1978.

Kamien, Janet. *What If You Couldn't...? A Book About Special Needs,* New York: Charles Scribner's Sons, 1979.

Sense Ability. From Regional Rehabilitation Research Institute on Attitudinal, Legal and Leisure Barriers, 1828 L. Street, N.W., Suite 704, Washington, DC 20036.

Statistics from *Sense Ability.*

MOBILITY IMPAIRMENT

It is estimated that about 25 million Americans have orthopedic or mobility impairments. Of these, one million are children. Approximately 500,000 persons who have mobility impairments use wheelchairs. Others use crutches, braces, walkers, and canes or move about without special support aids. Wheelchairs come in many sizes and shapes, which are adapted to the lifestyle of the user and increase the user's mobility. They range from basic utility models for use in hospitals and airports, to custom designed models for sports activities. There are also motorized electric wheelchairs that are battery operated. The two basic types of crutches used are the underarm crutch, or auxiliary crutch, and the forearm Canadian, or Lofstrand, crutch. Braces are used for support and balance. They can be made of metal or plastic.

They are hinged at the joints to allow movement of the knee and hip. Some attach directly to the shoe while others strap on. Wearing braces sometimes minimizes pressure on bones.

Many orthopedic disabilities require medical care, especially for growing children. Adjustments and changes in mobility devices require a medical person's prescription. However, orthopedic impairments are not contagious and should not be thought of as illnesses.

The greatest handicap for people with mobility impairments is the physical and attitudinal barriers imposed by society, because both attitudinal and architectural barriers keep people with disabilities from full participation in society. Therefore, public laws have been enacted to mandate specifications for making buildings and facilities accessible to and usable by people with disabilities. For a building to be accessible for a person using a wheelchair, exterior and interior space must be considered. A person must be able to get into the building, get around the building once inside, and be able to use the bathrooms, water fountains, telephones, and elevator buttons. The following must be considered: the use of ramps for abrupt changes in levels and steps; curb cuts at pedestrian crossings; uneven surfaces; narrow heavy doors; and any space that is too small to maneuver a wheelchair, such as corridors, bathrooms, and doorways. Water fountains, public telephones, and elevator buttons must be at a height that can be reached from a sitting position.

Wheelchairs used by adults vary in width from 27 to 32 inches. Doors should have a 32-inch clear opening to allow people using wheelchairs (or with braces, walkers, and crutches) to pass through. The average reach of a person seated in a wheelchair is between 48 and 54 inches.

Barnes, Ellen, Berrigan, Carol, and Biklen, Douglas. *What's the Difference: Teaching Positive Attitudes Toward People with Disabilities*, Syracuse, NY: Human Policy Press, 1978.

Free Wheeling. From Regional Rehabilitation Research Institute on Attitudinal, Legal and Leisure Barriers, 1828 L. St., N.W., Suite 704, Washington, DC 20036.

Kamien, Janet. *What If You Couldn't...? A Book About Special Needs.* New York: Charles Scribner's Sons, 1979.

Statistics quoted from *Free Wheeling.*

LEGAL DEFINITION OF DISABILITY

The legal definition of disability, taken from Section 834.J of the Federal Register Final Regulations to Implement Section 504 of the Rehabilitation Act of 1973 reads as follows:

"Handicapped person" means any person who (i) has a physical or mental impairment which substantially limits one or more major life activities, (ii) has a record of such an impairment, or (iii) is regarded as having such an impairment.

"Physical or mental impairment" means (a) any physiological disorder or condition, cosmetic disfigurement, or anatomical loss affecting one or more of the following body systems: neurological; musculoskeletal; special sense organs; respiratory, including speech organs; cardiovascular; reproductive; digestive; genito-urinary; hemic and lymphatic; skin; and endocrine; or (b) any mental or psychological disorder, such as mental retardation, organic brain syndrome, emotional or mental illness, and specific learning disabilities.

"Major life activities" means functions such as: caring for one's self, performing manual tasks, walking, seeing, hearing, speaking, breathing, learning, and working.

"Has a record of such an impairment" means has a history of, or has been classified as having, mental or physical impairment that substantially limits one or more major life activities.

"Is regarded as having an impairment" means (a) has physical or mental impairment that does not substantially limit major life activities but that is treated . . . as constituting such a limitation; (b) has a physical or mental impairment that substantially limits major life activities only as a result of the attitudes of others toward such an impairment; or (c) has none of the impairments but is treated as having such an impairment.

It should become apparent from this definition that: disability is not always visible; it's important to recognize the continuum and breadth of disabilities; many people have conditions defined as disabilities while eschewing the "disabled" label because of its negative connotations.

About the Authors

Merle Froschl is co-director of Educational Equity Concepts, Inc., a national nonprofit organization she co-founded with Barbara Sprung in 1982. From 1980-1982, Ms. Froschl was director of the Non-Sexist Child Development Project where she directed Project R.E.E.D. (Resources on Educational Equity for the Disabled) and Beginning Equal: The Project on Nonsexist Childrearing for Infants and Toddlers. From 1973-1979, Merle Froschl was director of educational services at The Feminist Press and editor of the second edition of *Feminist Resources for Schools and Colleges: A Guide to Curricular Materials*. She also was field testing director of the "Women's Lives/Women's Work" series. Ms. Froschl has a Bachelor of Arts degree in Journalism from Syracuse University and has written extensively on issues of educational equity for professional journals and the popular press. She has conducted inservice training, given workshop presentations, and lectured widely at conferences and professional meetings for more than a dozen years. Most recently, she was director of Project Inclusive, co-coordinator of the Women and Disability Awareness Project, and one of the authors of *Building Community: A Manual Exploring Issues of Women and Disability*.

Linda Colón is the general administrator for Educational Equity Concepts, Inc. where she also was the administrative coordinator for Project Inclusive and took an active role in the development and pilot testing of the curricular activities. Prior to joining the staff of Educational Equity Concepts in December 1983, Ms. Colón was Administrative Assistant for the Non-Sexist Child Development Project of the Women's Action Alliance, Inc. While there, she was administrative assistant for Project R.E.E.D. (Resources on Educational Equity for the Disabled) and coordinator of Access to Equality: The First National Conference on Educational Equity for Disabled Women and Girls. Ms. Colón also has worked in several administrative capacities for city and state agencies, including the New York State Women's Division, Hunter College, and the New York City Board of Higher Education. She was on the planning committee for Women, Education, and Work, a conference sponsored by the New York City Board of Education. At present, in addition to her work at Educational Equity Concepts, Inc., Linda Colón is a member of the National Conference of Puerto Rican Women, New York Chapter, where she has been editor of the newsletter and has served on the Board of Directors. She is presently working toward her Bachelor of Science degree in Psychology at Hunter College, CUNY.

Ellen Rubin has been involved in the education of children and adults with disabilities since 1967, when she graduated from Washington College in Maryland with a Bachelor of Arts in Psychology. Ms. Rubin also has conducted inservice and preservice training for teachers and other professionals as well as workshops for students of all ages. During the years from 1969 to 1980, Ellen Rubin both worked in Israel and received her Masters in Special Education from the Bank Street College of Education. While in Israel she worked at the George Simmons Rehabilitation Center for the Blind in Beersheva with children, adolescents, and their families. Ms. Rubin was educational program coordinator, developed a mainstreaming program for preschool children, and planned and implemented a paraprofessional training program. In 1980, Ellen Rubin returned to the United States to be Educational Programming Counselor at the Association for the Advancement of the Blind and Retarded, Inc. in Jamaica, New York and then worked as a special educator in an Early Intervention Program with infants and toddlers ages birth to three who were developmentally delayed at the Guild for Exceptional Children in Brooklyn, New York. From December 1983 to the present, Ms. Rubin has been staff specialist at Educational Equity Concepts, Inc. where she was a member of the team that developed and pilot tested the Project Inclusive curriculum. She also is a member of the Commissioner's Advisory Panel for the Education of Children with Handicapping Conditions for the New York State Education Department.

Barbara Sprung was the founding director, in 1972, of the Non-Sexist Child Development Project at the Women's Action Alliance, Inc. Since that time, Ms. Sprung has been a pioneer in the development of early childhood programs and materials that are nonsexist, multicultural, and inclusive of images of children and adults with disabilities. She was responsible for the development of My Family and Community Helpers block accessory figures, Play Scenes lotto, First Readings About My Family and My School, Community Career Flannel Board, People at Work and Men in Nurturing Roles photo sets, and Resource Photos for Mainstreaming. She is a much sought-after speaker and has written extensively for journals and popular magazines. She is the author of *Non-Sexist Education for Young Children: A Practical Guide* and *Creating a New Mainstream: An Early Childhood Training Manual for an "Inclusionary" Curriculum,* and was editor of *Perspectives on Non-Sexist Early Childhood Education.* In 1982, Barbara Sprung co-founded Educational Equity Concepts, Inc. with Merle Froschl and also has been its co-director. She participated in the development and implementation of Project Inclusive and was director of Beginning Math and Science Equitably. Ms. Sprung received a Bachelor of Arts in Early Childhood Education from Sarah Lawrence College and a Masters in Child Development from Bank Street College of Education.

About Educational Equity Concepts, Inc.

Educational Equity Concepts, Inc. is a national, nonprofit organization founded in 1982 to foster the development of children and adults through advancing educational excellence and equity. The organization creates educational programs and materials that are free of sex, race, and disability bias; offers training programs for parents, teachers, and students; and engages in a variety of public education activities.

One of our basic philosophical tenets is to "begin at the beginning." To this end, we are engaged in a variety of early childhood projects. Currently, our early childhood programs emphasize math, science, and mainstreaming, and we are developing classroom resources such as block accessories and curriculum guides.

Educational Equity Concepts also is concerned with maximizing the opportunities of adults who have not had the chance to "begin early." In this area, we focus on programs to help women with disabilities and women of color achieve educational equity and develop their full potential.

In all of our programs, Educational Equity Concepts's approach is "inclusive," making the connections between various factors that can limit individual growth and potential. *Including All of Us: An Early Childhood Curriculum About Disability* is a direct result of that endeavor. We believe that by making a classroom nonsexist, multicultural, and accessible to children with disabilities, it becomes a better environment for all children.